The

YOUR FAMILY NAME

Family's
First Bible Storybook

"These commandments that I give you today are to be upon your hearts. Impress them on your children. Talk about them when you sit at home and when you walk along the road, and when you lie down and when you get up." Deuteronomy 6:6,7, *(NIV)*

Date: _____

Family Members: *Birth Dates:*

Special Dates/Events
We Want to Remember:

Photos/Notes
About Our Family

OUR FAMILY'S FIRST BIBLE STORYBOOK

Regal Books

A Division of GL Publications
Ventura, California, U.S.A.

ETHEL BARRETT

The stories in this book have been recorded on audiocassettes by Ethel Barrett and include self-directing activities for children with each story.

Published by Regal Books
A Division of GL Publications
Ventura, California 93006
Printed in U.S.A.

Except where otherwise indicated Scripture quotations in this book are from:
NIV—Holy Bible: The New International Version Copyright © 1973, 1978, 1984 by the International Bible Society. Used by permission of Zondervan Bible Publishers.

Also quoted is:
ICB—International Children's Bible, New Century Version, copyright © 1986 by Sweet Publishing, Fort Worth, Texas 76137. Used by permission.

Library of Congress Cataloging-in-Publication Data

Barrett, Ethel.
    Our family's first Bible storybook.

    Summary: Presents a collection of Old and New Testament stories. Includes two finger puppets to use with the puppet dialogue that follows each story.
    1. Bible stories, English. [1. Bible stories. 2. Puppets] I. Title.
BS551.2.B318   1987   220.9′505   87-26376
ISBN 0-8307-1217-8

1 2 3 4 5 6 7 8 9 10 / 91 90 89 88 87

Rights for publishing this book in other languages are contracted by Gospel Literature International (GLINT) foundation. GLINT also provides technical help for the adaptation, translation, and publishing of Bible study resources and books in scores of languages worldwide. For further information, contact GLINT, Post Office Box 488, Rosemead, California, 91770, U.S.A., or the publisher.

Stories in This Book

Hi, Boys and Girls!

These are stories about some of the important people in the Bible—from the very beginning to the very end. All kinds of stories—long stories, short stories, and all the sizes in between. And all kinds of people! Good ones and bad ones, noisy ones and quiet ones, brave ones and cowardly ones, kind ones and MEAN ones.

This book will tell you how they lived and what they did and why. And it will make you think of what YOU might have done if you'd been faced with the same problems they were.

And to HELP you think, here's Mike and Tracy.

What? You haven't met Mike and Tracy? Well, then, let me introduce you!

Mike and Tracy are puppets. The kind you slip over your finger and make them turn their heads every which way, and wiggle and jiggle and nod yes or no—or even hop up and down in joy or anger, if that's how they feel.

Now then, Mike and Tracy talk about the people in the stories, and about their own lives, too.

And when THEY run out of things to say—you can add your own ideas of what they should say so you can keep them talking. And who knows? YOUR ideas may be even better than the ones you find in this book!

Try it! It's FUN!

A Note to Teachers and Parents

The puppet dialogues in this book are only a springboard, something to "get you started" in discussing these stories. As you read each dialogue, your children can use their puppets to act it out. Before long, your children will enjoy adding their own thoughts. And you may be in for a surprise. Children are both witty and profound, and have their own brand of wisdom and insight—in fact, you may find yourself learning as much as you teach!

My heartfelt thanks to my editor, Frances Blankenbaker. Her splendid academic background and incisive insight are exceeded only by her impeccable tact. She would do well in the diplomatic service. But her greatest talent is for getting to the heart of a problem without interfering with a writer's style, and without spoiling the poetic rhythm that is so necessary in writing for children.

The idea of having puppets was hers. I wrote the dialogue reluctantly at first, then realized it was not only a splendid teaching tool, but fun!

Joyce Thimsen, Stacey Martin, Gil Beers, Tim Howard and Frances procured the marvelous photography, some from their private collections, some taken on location especially for these stories. They not only thought of the ideas, but implemented them.

I heartily thank them all!

It Didn't Just Happen!

Once there was a world. And it didn't just happen. It was made. It was made according to a PLAN.

In the very beginning of the Bible it tells us that God made the world. And He didn't make it just any old way either. He put everything in its place and it was all JUST RIGHT. And this is what He did.

The first thing God did was make the light. He made it by just SAYING, "Let there be light." God tells us so in the Bible. He separated the light from the darkness, and He called the light "day." And He called the darkness "night." But the world wasn't finished yet. It needed more. And God DID more.

The second day He said, "Let there be a sky." And there was! He stretched it out overhead, blue and beautiful. The Bible says that God stretched out the sky like a curtain. So now the world had day and night—and a sky. But it wasn't finished yet. It needed more. Do you know why? It was all water! Everywhere, all over, every BIT of it was water. Now of course THAT wasn't the way God wanted it. It needed MUCH more than that. And God DID more.

The third day God gathered the water together and separated it from the land. Oh there was a LOT of water. Enough to make great big oceans. Enough to make rivers and lakes. And enough left over to make little creeks. God put the oceans and the rivers and the lakes and the creeks right where He wanted them. And He made them stay right there in their places. He even made the mighty ocean stay in its place, just as if it were a baby. "This far you may go," He said, "and this far—but no farther." And the ocean has been obeying God ever since, which is a very good thing, when you stop to think that if the ocean just BURPS, we have a tidal wave.

Then God spoke to the seeds that He had put into the dry land, and He said, "Grow." And they did! Some grew just to make things beautiful—like the lovely flowers and trees and grass and vines. And some grew things to eat—like vegetables and fruits and nuts and berries. Of course most things grew UP—like corn and tomatoes and oranges and peas. But some things grew DOWN— like carrots and radishes. And some things grew SIDEWAYS—like vines creeping along the ground. But everything grew in SOME direction. And the earth began to look very beautiful.

On the fourth day, God hung out the sun and He hung out the moon and He hung out the stars. Oh that was a wonderful day! God tells us in the Bible that the "stars sang together for joy." God put each star in its own pathway, and He said, "Now, don't you get in the way of any other star." And the stars obeyed God, and each little star stayed in its own pathway. And God hung out the sun to shine in the daytime and the moon to shine at night. That was really a wonderful day.

At last God had finished nearly everything He wanted to make. The light and the darkness. The sky and the sun and the moon and the stars. The oceans and rivers and lakes and creeks. The dry land, the flowers and trees and vegetables and fruits.

After all these things were made, God looked at the beautiful world and He said, "It is GOOD."

That means it was JUST RIGHT.

Tracy and Mike Talk It Over

Mike: Do you know that the sun is more than a million times bigger than the earth? And that the nearest star is about twenty-four TRILLION miles away?

Tracy: Do you know what a galaxy is? I learned it in school.

Mike: Sure. It's a group of stars. And there are ten thousand galaxies racing through space—

Tracy: More than that, my Dad told me. They keep discovering new ones.

Mike: And they don't bump into each other! How does that grab you?

Tracy: What d'you mean, how does that "grab" me?

Mike: How does that make you feel?

Tracy: It makes me feel *little*. But if God could make the world "just right" He can sure take care of me.

Mike: Yes, and if He can keep the stars from bumping into each other, He can keep me from chasing a ball into the street and bumping into a car.

Tracy: Can you think of some other ways He takes care of us?

Let your puppets take it from here.

Some Bible Verses to Learn

In the beginning God created the heavens and the earth.
Genesis 1:1
Ah, Sovereign LORD, you have made the heavens and the earth by your great power and outstretched arm. Nothing is too hard for you.
Jeremiah 32:17

Talk to God

Thank God that He made the world just right. Thank Him for taking care of you. Think of some special way in which He has cared for you and tell Him you appreciate it.

Can You Find This Story in the Bible?

Find Genesis 1:1-19; Job 38:7; Isaiah 40:22

The
First Man

God had made a wonderful world! Everything He had made was just right. The light and the darkness. The sky and the moon and the stars. The oceans and rivers and lakes. The dry land, and the flowers and trees and vegetables and fruit. This was a wonderful world—

Except for one thing.

There were no living creatures in it!

There was all that water—and no fish to swim in it.

And all that beautiful sky—and no birds to fly in it.

And all those forests and fields and hills and valleys— and no animals to run and climb and play in them.

And this is what God did.

First He made the fishes. ALL the fishes. More fishes than you can even dream of!

Tiny goldfishes and guppies—

and middle-sized fishes—

and GREAT BIG fishes—

like WHALE-SHARKS!

God said, "Let the oceans and lakes and rivers and creeks be FILLED with all kinds of fishes."

And they were!

The tiny fishes swam in the little brooks. The middle-sized fishes swam in the lakes and rivers. And EVERY kind of fish swam in the big oceans, from tiny ones to whale-sharks as long as some of our houses.

God made the fishes but that wasn't all. The next thing He made—was birds. So many birds! More birds than you can imagine!

Tiny humming-birds
 and middle-sized birds—
  and GREAT BIG birds—
  like EAGLES and FLAMINGOS and
  PEACOCKS and even OSTRICHES!

And God said, "Let the birds fly across the sky—all over the earth!"

And they did!

Some birds flew around the trees and stayed in the little hills and valleys. Some birds—like the sea gulls—flew out over the water. And some BIG birds—like the eagle—flew to the highest mountaintops!

Now God had made the fishes and the birds, but STILL that wasn't all. The NEXT thing He made—was animals. More animals than you can even think of!

Little mice and chipmunks—
 And middle-sized dogs and pigs—
  and GREAT BIG BEARS and LIONS and TIGERS and
  even ELEPHANTS!

God said, "Let there be all kinds of animals—big ones and little ones and all sizes in between. And let them roam all over the earth."

And they did!

Some animals—like the alligator—stayed near the water. Some—like the monkeys—climbed the trees. And some just liked to get way off by themselves in the deep forest.

Now this was all very wonderful. Except for one thing.

There was nobody for God to talk to. Nobody to talk back to Him. Nobody in all this world for God to love with a SPECIAL love—and enjoy forever! So the next thing God did was the most wonderful of all. He said, "Let Us create MAN in our own image."

15

And that's exactly what He did!

God created man, and He called this man ADAM.

God let Adam live in this wonderful world. He let Adam take care of all the beautiful things. And He even let Adam give all the animals and birds their names! The Bible says that God brought all the beasts and the birds to Adam to see what he would call them. Adam named every bird, from the tiny hummingbirds to the great big peacocks. And every animal from the tiny chipmunks to the great big elephants. He gave every living creature its name!

Yes, Adam was created to care for all that God had made. But most important of all, God had somebody He could love with a SPECIAL love. And Adam loved God.

After all these things were done, God said, "It is good."

That means everything was JUST RIGHT.

Just the way the world was made. According to a plan. Just right. That's the way God made the things IN the world.

Just right.

Tracy and Mike Talk It Over

Mike: It's hard to believe that God wanted Adam to talk to Him.

Tracy: I know it. You wouldn't think that God would ever need anything or anybody.

Mike: But He does. He wants US.

Tracy: And He actually wants us to TALK to Him.

Mike: What if I don't have anything to say? Some days I don't.

Tracy: I read a story once about a boy who used to begin his prayers with "God—this is Jimmy." And then he'd talk to God. Or if he couldn't think of anything to say he'd just stay there and be quiet like he was listening.

Mike: Sometimes maybe God just wants us to be with Him whether we say anything or not.

Tracy: Sure! We can just be quiet and listen. Or we can thank Him for things.

Mike: Or ask Him for things!

Tracy: And we can pray for other people!

Have your puppets take it from here. Encourage them to think of specific things they can pray about.

A Bible Verse to Learn

Know that the LORD is God. It is he who made us, and we are his; we are his people, the sheep of his pasture. Psalm 100:3

Talk to God

Thank God that He wants to talk to you. And that He loves to have you listen to Him. Tell Him your name. Tell him about your day. Ask Him to help you to be stronger, kinder—or maybe to swat a ball better in Little League. He cares about *everything*.

Can You Find This Story in the Bible?

Find Genesis 1:20-31; Genesis 2:1-3,7,9,19,20.

The
First Lie

God had been so good to Adam! He had made a wonderful
world that was "just right." And He had given Adam a
beautiful garden to live in. There were no signs that said "KEEP
OFF THE GRASS" and no signs that said "DO NOT FEED THE
ANIMALS." Adam could do anything he pleased—except ONE
THING. He could not eat the fruit of ONE CERTAIN TREE. This
tree was in the middle of the garden. God knew it was best for
Adam not to eat the fruit on this tree. He TOLD Adam. "Adam,"
He said, "this is the tree of the knowledge of good and evil, and if
you eat that fruit, it will HURT you." Well THAT'S plain enough!

God had done MANY things for Adam, but He asked Adam to
do just ONE thing for Him—to OBEY Him.

And God thought of everything to make Adam happy. He even
made Adam a beautiful wife, and her name was Eve. So now Adam
had the garden, the animals and the birds—and a wife!

Adam and Eve were so happy in the garden—it didn't seem
possible that anything could go wrong.

But something did. And it happened like this:

One day, Eve was walking in the garden, when she came to the
tree right in the middle—the tree that God had said not to eat

from. Eve was looking at the fruit and thinking about it, when along came—a beautiful creature. This beautiful creature was a serpent.

And the serpent said to Eve, "Has God said that you must not eat the fruit from EVERY tree in the garden?"

"Oh NO," said Eve. "God didn't say that at all. We can eat all the OTHER fruit. It's just the fruit on this ONE TREE that we should not eat. God said it would hurt us."

And that wicked serpent told the lie that started all the trouble. "It won't REALLY hurt you." he said slyly. "It will just make you WISE. You shall be as gods, knowing good and evil."

Well!

It SOUNDED so good that Eve believed it.

First she picked some fruit. Then she ATE it.

Then she gave Adam some. And HE ate it, too.

And so they both disobeyed God.

Well, the MINUTE they disobeyed God, they began to be afraid. When God came to visit them, and they heard His voice in the garden, they were so afraid that they HID.

"Adam," called God, "where are you?"

And Adam called back, "Lord, I was afraid when I heard your voice, and so I hid."

Now of course Adam and Eve couldn't REALLY hide from God. God knew right where they were. And He also knew that they had done the ONE THING He had told them NOT to do.

And because they had disobeyed Him, God told Adam and Eve to leave the garden.

God still LOVED Adam and Eve. He loved them so much that He even went with them outside the garden, to watch over them.

But nothing could be quite the same again. God had made a beautiful garden—but Adam and Eve had disobeyed—and spoiled it all!

The Bible tells us that ALL of us have sinned—we have ALL disobeyed God. But the Bible also has some wonderful news! And that news is for YOU! First there's something you must do. The Bible tells us what in Psalm 38:18: "I confess my guilt. I am troubled by my sin" *(ICB)*.

And now comes the wonderful news. God has already sent His Son Jesus to take your punishment! All you have to do is BELIEVE that. And then let Him KNOW you believe it. Tell Him you want to belong to Him. For the Bible says that "God so loved the world [that means you] that he gave his one and only Son, that whoever [that means you again] BELIEVES in him shall . . . have eternal life" (John 3:16). After you've done this, do you know who you are? Why, you're a child of God! Isn't THAT wonderful news?

Tracy and Mike Talk It Over

Tracy: Do you believe God sent Jesus to take your punishment?

Mike: Sure I do. And I've told Him so. And I've told Him I want to belong to Him, too.

Tracy: Have you ever said it aloud? To other people?

Mike: Well, yes, to my mom and dad. And to my Sunday School teacher.

Tracy: Would you be able to tell all that to somebody else? What would you say? My dad says if you can explain all this, you'll know more than most grown-ups.

Let your puppets take it from here. (Parent/teacher: the children may need prompting. Go over the "wonderful news" line by line and have them explain each step in their own words.)

A Bible Verse to Learn

Yet to all who received him, to those who believed in his name, he gave the right to become children of God. John 1:12

Talk to God

Thank God for sending Jesus to be your Saviour. Ask Him to show you the wrong things you do. And to help you not to do them again. Thank Him for loving you so much.

Can You Find This Story in the Bible?

Find Genesis 3:1-24.

The Strangest Boat in the World

There is one thing God wants, more than anything else in the world. He wants His children to love and obey Him.

He does!

Remember, Adam and Eve didn't obey God and they had to leave the beautiful garden. But that wasn't all—

Adam and Eve had children, and their children had children, until after awhile—oh, it took a long time—but after awhile, the world was just FILLED with people who didn't obey God. NO ONE obeyed God—

Except for one man. He still talked to God, and prayed to God, and thanked God for everything. And he taught his family to know God and obey Him, too! His name was Noah, and he had quite a family. He had a wife—Mrs. Noah; and three sons, and their wives—and their names were

Mr. and Mrs. Shem,

And Mr. and Mrs. Ham,

And Mr. and Mrs. Japheth.

Now one day, Noah called his family around him, and he said, "Something very important is going to happen. God has been talking to me, and He has given me some plans."

"Plans?" said Noah's family. "What plans? Are they for a house? Are they for a castle?"

"No," said Noah. "They're not for a house. And they're not for a castle. They're for a BOAT. God calls it an ARK."

"An ark?" they cried. "An ARK?" They could hardly believe their ears. "Why there isn't even any WATER around here. Why would God want you to build an ark?"

"God is very sad," said Noah. "And He's told me something that's very sad. God has told me that all the people are so wicked, that His beautiful world is spoiled. And He's going to have to destroy it. He's going to send a big flood."

A flood? A FLOOD?

Why, that was hard to believe. It was even hard to IMAGINE. Noah and his family just had to take God's word for it, and obey.

And they did.

They began to build a boat.

Now this was no ordinary job. It was a BIG job. For this was no ordinary boat. It was a BIG boat. It was bigger than that, even. It was TREMENDOUS!

This ark had to be big enough for Noah and his whole family—and that wasn't all!

It had to be big enough to hold hundreds of animals and birds, and enough food to last for a long, long time.

Noah and his helpers got to work. They cut down big trees. They measured. They sawed—zzz-schhhh-zzzz-schhhh. They fit pieces together. They hammered. They lifted and hammered some more—until they had built that great ark exactly as God had told them to.

It was three stories high.

Almost as big as a battleship.

And it had a window, way up high, big enough so that plenty of air could get in.

Yes, building the ark was a big job, and it took a long time. But finally, the ark was done.

People came to look at it, and went on their way again. They didn't care about the old ark, and they didn't care about God. And they didn't care about Noah. If they thought about him at all, it was to laugh at him.

But Noah didn't care.

He didn't care because he was busy obeying God. He didn't care if PEOPLE laughed. He knew GOD was pleased.

Because there is one thing God wants more than anything else. He wants His children to love Him and obey Him.

And that's just what Noah and his family had done.

Tracy and Mike Talk It Over

Tracy: Boy, Noah was the only one in the whole world who was obeying God. Noah and his family.

Mike: Have YOU ever felt you were all alone—the only one obeying?

Tracy: A couple of times. And the kids at school laughed at me.

Mike: How did it make you feel?

Tracy: I didn't like it one bit! I felt lonely. Did this ever happen to you?

Mike: Sure, once. The kids were going down the street to a house that was just being built. They were going to jump off things and fool around. And they laughed at me because I wouldn't go.

Tracy: You wouldn't go because you wanted to obey God?

Mike: You BET I wanted to obey God. 'Cause I fooled around like that in an empty house once. And I broke my arm. God taught me a lesson.

Have your puppets take it from here.

Prompt them to tell times when they've obeyed even when others did not, and why.

A Bible Verse to Learn

We must obey God rather than men! Acts 5:29

Talk to God

Thank God for caring about you. Thank Him for knowing how you feel when you're obeying and nobody else is. Ask Him to help you stick to doing what's right even if the others are laughing at you.

Can You Find This Story in the Bible?

Find Genesis 6:1-22.

The Strangest Boat Ride in the World

Noah obeyed God.

The ark that God had told Noah to make, was finished. And now Noah was ready to begin the NEXT step of his important job. And if building the huge ark was hard, this next step was even harder.

For God had told him to gather animals to put in the ark. Not just any old animals. And not just a FEW animals. But a father and a mother of EVERY KIND of animal in the land. And that wasn't all.

Noah had to gather FOURTEEN of certain special animals. And that wasn't all.

He had to have food and water enough for all the animals and for his family, too.

Believe me, that meant a lot of animals and a lot of food. It was a BIG job.

Well, Noah did exactly as God had told him to do. He took two mice, two dogs, two lions, two elephants—

Two hummingbirds, two robins, two peacocks, Two—

From the littlest to the biggest, there wasn't one single kind of animal or bird or insect left out.

That wasn't easy!

But at last everything was ready. And then—

God told Noah and his family—

    Mrs. Noah—

        Mr. and Mrs. Shem—

            Mr. and Mrs. Ham—

                and Mr. and Mrs. Japheth—

—to go into the ark, and to bring with them all the animals and all the birds that they had gathered together.

Now it hadn't started to rain yet. But Noah didn't wait around to see if it would rain. He obeyed God. The Bible tells us that THE SAME DAY Noah entered the ark with his family. And all the animals! What a sight that must have been!

Two chipmunks, two pigs, two tigers, two sparrows, two eagles, two monkeys, two giraffes, two pigeons, two squirrels, two—

From the littlest to the BIGGEST, two of every kind. And fourteen of certain SPECIAL kinds. That line of animals just went on and on and on and on and ON.

It took a long time. But after a while Noah and his family and the animals were all safe in the ark. And then—

The Bible says, "God shut the door." And THEN—

Nothing happened. Absolutely nothing. Nothing happened and nothing happened and nothing happened. For seven whole days. And then—

RAIN!

Noah and his family heard the first sprinkles on the roof of the ark. Then they heard the rain coming down

    harder

        and harder

            and HARDER.

The water began to slosh up along the bottom of the ark. It sloshed and sloshed and got deeper and DEEPER. And then that great big ark CREAKED—and SWAYED a bit—and then—

It—began—to—FLOAT.

It was going to be all right. Noah had followed every single direction in the plans God had given him, and the ark was watertight, and balanced right, and seaworthy.

The ark floated there in the clearing for several days. The rain came down day and night. On and on and on.

Inside the ark, Noah and his family had plenty to do. They took care of the animals and fed them, and they kept the ark clean. And every day they prayed, and thanked God for keeping them safe.

And that water got higher and HIGHER. After a while, only the treetops showed above the water. And after a long while, even the MOUNTAIN tops were covered with water, and there was nothing left but water and sky. By this time, it had rained forty days and forty nights.

And then the rain stopped.

Now Noah didn't know what was going to happen next. Neither did Mrs. Noah. Nor Mr. and Mrs. Shem. Nor Mr. and Mrs. Ham.

Nor Mr. and Mrs. Japheth. No one knew. But they weren't afraid.

They weren't afraid, because they DID know one thing. They had done exactly what God had told them to do. And God would keep them safe, for they had OBEYED.

Tracy and Mike Talk It Over

Mike: Boy! Noah had to get ready for what God said was going to happen when it hadn't even happened yet!

Tracy: If you were walking along a path with your dad and he suddenly shouted, "STOP!" would you stop?

Mike: I sure would!

Tracy: Why would you?

Mike: Because I trust my dad. Maybe there is danger ahead.

Tracy: Can you think of any things your parents have warned you about? Even if they haven't happened yet?

Mike: Not to speak to strangers—

Tracy: Or get in their cars—

Have your puppets take it from here. Depending on the children's age, prompt them to discuss hidden dangers—smoking, taking strange pills, etc.

A Bible Verse to Learn

The rules you commanded are right and completely trustworthy.
Psalm 119:138, *ICB*

Talk to God

Thank God for warning you about dangers ahead. Noah was safe only if he obeyed God and got into the ark. Ask God to help you to obey even if you don't understand WHY.

Can You Find This Story in the Bible?

Find Genesis 7:1-24.

Noah Says, "Thank You"

Next to loving Him and obeying Him, one thing God wants His children to do is THANK Him.

And Noah and his family had plenty to thank God for. For even though there was absolutely nothing outside but water—they were safe and snug inside the ark.

Days went by. Weeks went by. Months went by. Three months. Four months. Five months! And then, finally—

Wind!

Wind. Howling outside the ark. Racing across the water. Driving the water away. Making it go down faster. God hadn't forgotten them!

Indeed He hadn't. The Bible says, "And God REMEMBERED Noah and his family and all the animals that were with him in the ark; and God made a wind to pass over the earth, and the waters began to go down."

The waters went down and down and down and DOWN—until, one day—the great ark creaked and s-c-r-a-p-e-d—and—settled down and—came to a stop. It had landed on a high mountaintop!

It was time to get busy at last. First Noah took a raven and let him out the window. But the raven never came back. Then Noah let a little dove out the window. The dove flew back and forth across the waters, and then came back!

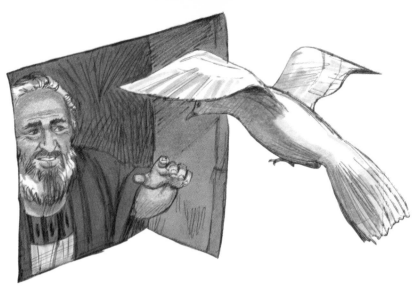

A week later Noah let the little dove out the window again. She flew across the waters—and disappeared. But that evening she came back. And in her beak was a leaf from an olive tree! That meant the water had gone down below the treetops.

A week later, Noah let the little dove out the window again. This time she never came back. And they knew she had probably found a tree to build a nest in, and that most of the water had gone.

Noah and his sons got to work. They took the covering off the ark so they could look out. Most of the water HAD gone. But they still waited for God to tell them to leave the ark.

And in a few weeks, God DID tell them.

What a day THAT was!

The great ark door opened with a C-R-E-A-K. And out came Noah and his family.

And all the animals!

The animals acted all different ways. The brave ones, like the lions, made a dash for the forest. The timid ones, like the kittens, walked around in little circles, not quite sure what to do.

But Noah knew there was one thing HE wanted to do before he did anything else. He wanted to thank God. So the first thing he did was to gather some stones and pile them up and make an altar. And there Noah and his family knelt down and worshiped God and thanked Him for saving them.

And God made Noah a VERY IMPORTANT promise. God said, "I will never again destroy the earth with a flood. And just so you'll remember, I will give you a sign. Every time it rains I'll put a rainbow in the sky. And when I see that rainbow I'll remember my promise."

And it turned out just as God had said. Every time it rained, sure enough, up in the sky was the most beautiful rainbow—just like a big curved bridge—shining with all its colors!

And Noah and his family were happy because God had kept them safe.

But most of all, God was pleased because Noah had remembered to thank Him.

Tracy and Mike Talk It Over

Tracy: Are you thankful for all the things you have?

Mike: I am now. I didn't used to be. I griped about almost EVERYthing. My dad told me once that I wasn't even thankful that I had a head. And my mom said I probably wished I had TWO heads so I could talk with my mouth full. That was supposed to be a joke. I didn't think it was funny then. But I do now.

Tracy: Things sure do go better when you remember to say thank you.

Mike: Do you think it really matters to God when you thank Him?

Tracy: The Bible says that God WANTS us to thank Him. It's a way we can show God we love Him.

Mike: Okay, what do we thank Him FOR? Think of some things. Have your puppets take it from here.

A Bible Verse to Learn

Give thanks to the LORD, for he is good. Psalm 107:1

Talk to God

First thank God for sending Jesus to be our Saviour. Then see how many other things you can think of to thank God for. Try to think of things you usually don't notice, like air and water and food and houses and things like that. And thank Him especially for His loving care.

Can You Find This Story in the Bible?

Find Genesis 8:10-22; 9:1-19.

The Strange Journey

It was while Abraham was sitting out doors looking up at the stars and talking to God that he got this absolutely SHOCKING news.

"Abraham," God said, "I want you to get up, pack up your duds and go to a far-away land which I will show you."

WHAAA—?

Why, Abraham lived in the city of Ur—and was it ever a BEAUTIFUL city! It had splashing fountains and palm trees that clattered and chattered in the wind and the people lived in comfortable two-story houses made of brick and plaster. There was plenty of room for all the mothers and fathers and children and servants—room for everybody. The children went to school and learned to read and write and do arithmetic and they laughed as they played and the babies squealed and squrgled.

And Abraham was rich. He had flocks and herds and goats and camels and donkeys—and he had gold and silver too. He had a father whose name was Terah and he had a wife whose name was Sarah, and he had a nephew whose name was Lot. He had dozens

of cousins and uncles and aunts—lots of friends, too. So he was perfectly happy living where he was.

Well, there was ONE thing wrong with the city of Ur—the people there did not love God. They didn't pray to God. They prayed to idols of wood and metal. Still—

"But a strange land far away, God?" Abraham cried, "I don't even know where it IS."

"I TOLD you I'd show you the way," God said.

So that was that. When God speaks to you like that, you don't argue.

So Abraham decided then and there to do what God said.

When he told his wife Sarah about it, she looked at him in amazement. "But where will we live?" she cried. "And how?"

"We'll live in tents."

Sarah knew that she must obey her husband, for she loved him dearly. But wander off to a faraway country and live in TENTS?

Now living in tents is great fun for a couple of weeks if you're on vacation, but living in tents for weeks or months or years? And saying good-bye to your family and friends when you might never come back? That was FRIGHTENING.

But they did it!

What a lot of packing there was to do! Abraham and Sarah and all their servants got to work. They packed dishes and pots and rugs and blankets and tents and all kinds of food and loaded them on camels and donkeys. Then they said good-bye to all their brothers and sisters and cousins and aunts and uncles and nephews and nieces— all except one NEPHEW. This nephew's name was Lot and Abraham and Sarah decided to take him along.

Off they went across the hot, sunny desert. Some of them rode on camels and some of them walked alongside, and some of them kept their cattle and sheep together. There were no signposts saying "NEW COUNTRY—159 MILES." And no highway patrol to flag down and ask which way to go. But Abraham knew that God

The city of Ur had a huge temple tower called a ziggurat (ZIG-u-rat), where people worshiped idols. The first photo shows some people climbing to the top of the huge ziggurat. The second photo shows the land of Ur today from the top of the ziggurat. In the background are ruins of the palace of the king and the temple of the moon goddess. In the days of Abraham, the Persian Gulf came up into the land making it green and fertile. The one true God told Abraham to leave Ur, where the people worshiped idols, and to go to a new land that God would show him. (Photos © Joyce Thimsen)

was their friend and was watching over them all. When the sun went down at night and the desert got cold they stopped and built a fire, got their supper, put up their tents and unrolled their blankets. Before they went to bed they thanked God for watching over them. And after they were all asleep, Abraham went out under the stars again and talked with God.

Abraham wasn't worried.

He knew they were going to reach the new land.

He knew because he was following God one step at a time and God was his friend.

Tracy and Mike Talk It Over

Tracy: Did you ever go someplace when you didn't know where you were going?

Mike: Well my dad usually knows where we're going. But one time he didn't and we went around in circles.

Tracy: So what happened?

Mike: Well then my mom took a map out of the glove compartment and they followed it, one step at a time. And after awhile we got to where we wanted to go.

Tracy: Just like Abraham! Only he didn't have a map. They didn't have maps in those days.

Mike: But he had God. That was even better. Can you think of any ways we can trust God when we don't know which way to go?

Tracy: Well my dad didn't know whether to take a new job once. It was in another city. So the whole family prayed and asked God—even us kids. And after awhile different things happened to show my dad that God wanted him to take the new job. So we all moved to the new city.

Have your puppets take it from here. Suggest times when they've had to make changes and follow God's directions—in their own family living, or perhaps in school.

A Bible Verse to Learn

Abraham believed God, . . . and he was called God's friend.
James 2:23

Talk to God

Thank God for being the kind of friend we can believe. And thank Him for giving you parents and teachers you can trust.

Can You Find This Story in the Bible?

Find Genesis 12:1-20; 13:1-4.

The Selfish Choice

God watched over Abraham and the people who were with him, just as He had promised. They had some humps and bumps and delays along the way, but finally—

There it was!

Just as God had promised and what a beautiful land it was. It was just like a picture—long rolling hills covered with grass like a green velvet carpet, and trees and flowers and all for Abraham and his family and Lot to live in.

The first thing they all did was to pile stones up and make an altar and then they knelt down and thanked God for keeping them safe. Then they unpacked their duds and began to settle down to live.

For a while it was just one wonderful day after another. Abraham grew richer and RICHER, and his herds of cattle and sheep grew bigger and BIGGER—and that was wonderful.

And Lot grew richer and RICHER—and his herds of cattle and sheep grew bigger and BIGGER—and that was wonderful too.

But there was one little problem.

When Abraham's servants took their cattle and sheep to a pasture to eat grass, LOT'S cattle were there. And when Lot's servants took their cattle to a pasture to eat grass, ABRAHAM'S cattle were there. And it wasn't long before they were all mixed up. There just wasn't enough room for everybody. And so the servants began to quarrel.

"This is OUR spot," Lot's servants would say.

"It is not—it is OUR spot," Abraham's servants would say. And they quarreled and pushed and shouted.

Then Abraham heard about it.

He knew that all that land was really his because God had given it to him. He could have told Lot to go back home, but he didn't.

Instead he took Lot up on a high hill where they could look down over all the land and he said, "Lot, let's not quarrel. There's plenty of land for both of us. We can divide it."

Now Abraham could have given Lot a little piece or a middle-sized piece of land and taken the rest for himself, because the land really belonged to him. But instead, he said, "Lot, YOU choose the land you want and I'll take what's left over."

And Lot could have been polite and remembered that it was his uncle's land in the first place, but he didn't. Instead he looked on one side where the grass was beautiful and there was a big river—and he looked on the OTHER side where there wasn't much grass and there was no river—and he pointed to the BEST side and said, "Uncle Abraham, I'll take THAT side."

And he did.

He took his family and his servants and his cattle and his sheep and moved down into the very best part of the land and·settled down there to live. Abraham and Sarah and their servants and all their cattle stayed in the hills and Abraham built another altar and thanked God for being his friend.

Abraham wasn't worried. He knew that he didn't have the best piece of land, but he knew that he had done the right thing.

And doing the right thing was what counted—with God.

Tracy and Mike Talk It Over

Mike: Boy! Lot was sure a selfish one. Do you think it was right for Abraham to let him get away with that?

Tracy: Well, I'm not so sure, but it looks like Abraham showed his love for God more than Lot did.

Mike: Well, I'm sure he did, but I still think that must have been a hard decision for him to make, letting Lot get away with having all the best land while he got stuck with the poorest land. I'm not so sure that I could do that. I wonder if I would ever have to do something like that.

Tracy: Well, just supposing you and some of your friends were going to pitch your pup tents in your yard.

Mike: It sure sounds like fun.

Tracy: But suppose some of your yard is grassy and level and maybe under a shade tree, but some of it is out in the sun and full of bare spots.

Mike: I think I'd get out there first and pitch my tent under the shade tree where there's grass.

Tracy: Now wait a minute—they're your GUESTS.

Mike: So I guess I'd have to give them first choice, wouldn't I?

Tracy: Well, I asked my dad about this and he said you should be kind to your guests and give them first choice, no matter what happens, and whether you like it or not.

Mike: Why do you suppose Abraham did this? He knew what Lot was like. He must have known that Lot would choose the best part.

Tracy: Well, my dad says that Abraham loved God and he KNEW that God would take care of him, no matter what happened.

Mike: Oh, I get it. If you love God and believe He will help you, it makes it easier to give the other guy the first choice—even if he takes the best part.

Tracy: That's right, that's what my dad said. Can you think of some other times when you can give the other person the first choice?

Have your puppets take it from here.

(Suggest ways in which children can give the other person the first choice—the first one to choose sides—the first one to choose a treat—the first one to choose an activity, etc.)

A Bible Verse to Learn

Do to others as you would have them do to you. Luke 6:31

Talk to God

Be honest with God. Tell Him that it isn't always easy to let somebody else have the first choice. And ask Him to help you to do what's right. And if you come out with second best, ask God to help you to be happy with what you did get. Don't forget to thank God for times when someone gives YOU first choice!

Can You Find This Story in the Bible?

Find Genesis 13:5-18; 14:1-24.

The Visitors Who Made a Promise

Well, Abraham might have been left with the poorest piece of land, but God had not forgotten him. Abraham grew richer and RICHER. His herds of sheep and cattle and camels and donkeys grew bigger and BIGGER, and as if that weren't enough—

God made Abraham a very important promise. God promised Abraham he would have so many children, they would be harder to count than the grains of sand on the seashore. Now God didn't mean that Abraham and Sarah would have that many CHILDREN, He meant that they would have children and then they'd have grandchildren and then they'd have great-grandchildren, and then they would have great-great-great-great-great-grandchildren—until finally down through the years, all these children and their children's children would become a GREAT NATION!

There was only one little hitch. Abraham and Sarah didn't HAVE ANY CHILDREN—not even one. They wanted children

In Bible lands today, some shepherds still live in tents. Abraham was a very rich man, and so his tent would have been much more beautiful than the one in the photo. (Photo © Stacey Martin)

more than anything else in the world. They knew that God would keep His promise all right, but WHEN? God said SOMEDAY—

But He didn't say WHEN.

Well, the years went by and Abraham and Sarah got to be middle-aged and they still didn't have any children. God even spoke to Abraham again and told him he would have so many children they would be harder to count than the stars in the sky. But more years went by and Abraham and Sarah got to be OLD, and still they didn't have any children. And more years went by, and MORE years went by—

And THEN!

One day Abraham was sitting in the doorway of his tent when he looked up and saw three men in the distance. They were coming right toward him. Abraham didn't know that they were the Lord and two angels, for they looked just like any other men.

He ran to meet them and invited them to come and rest in the shade. The men sat down to rest and Abraham went into the tent and told Sarah they had company.

Then everybody got busy! Servants brought the men water so they could wash for dinner, Sarah baked some cakes, Abraham's servants killed a calf and cooked the meat, and before you could say "ABRAHAM"—a wonderful dinner was ready!

And after dinner, they sat around and talked while Sarah stayed inside the tent and listened.

And that's when the wonderful thing happened.

The Lord said to Abraham, "Before the year is up, you and Sarah are going to have a son of your own. A baby boy."

Before the year was up! Not just SOMEDAY—but PRETTY SOON!

After the visitors had left, Abraham and Sarah talked together and they thought, a baby boy—all our own. Not just SOMEDAY—but within a year!

And sure enough, before a year was up Abraham and Sarah had a real live squirgling baby boy. He was fat and dimpled and beautiful.

The very first thing they did was to thank God for him and then they named him Isaac. And that means "laughter."

At first Isaac couldn't do much of anything. Then he learned to smile. Then he learned to wiggle his toes. Then he learned how to put his foot in his mouth, and then he learned how to creep and then he learned how to WALK.

And all the while Isaac was growing up, Abraham and Sarah never stopped thanking God for him. God had made a promise and it had taken a long long time but He had kept it.

Tracy and Mike Talk It Over

Mike: Well, it sure took God a long time to keep His promise, didn't it?

Tracy: It sure did. And it sure takes a long time for PEOPLE to keep their promises, and sometimes they never do. Suppose you had a friend who moved away and he promised to write to you, and you waited and waited and WAITED—and he never did. You waited and waited and WAITED, and maybe he never will.

Mike: Well, people don't always keep their promises, but God always does.

Tracy: Can you think of some promises God has made to us that He is surely going to keep?

Mike: Sure I can. God's promises are right here in the Bible. Here's one: God says, "I will help you" (Isaiah 41:13). Can you think of any more of God's promises?

Have your puppets take it from here.
(Suggest promises such as those in Hebrews 13:5; Jeremiah 33:3; Genesis 28:15.)

A Bible Verse to Learn

God is faithful. 1 Corinthians 10:13

Talk to God

Thank God that He always keeps His promises. Ask Him to help you to be patient when He does not answer your prayers right away.

Can You Find This Story in the Bible?

Find Genesis 13:14-18; 15:1-18; 18:1-16; 21:1-8.

The Girl
Who Was
Extra Kind

Why, Isaac grew and GREW. He grew to be a little boy, he
grew to be a big boy and before you could say "ABRAHAM
AND SARAH"—he grew to be a man and it was time for him to be
married.

So Abraham told his trusted servant (whose name was Eliezer)
to go back to the country where Abraham's relatives lived and find
Isaac a wife. "Don't find just any WIFE, Eliezer," said Abraham,
"Find just the RIGHT wife. Ask God to give you directions and find
a wife who is kind."

So Eliezer took camels and jewels and presents and food and
some other servants and went way back to the city where
Abraham's relatives lived. When they got there they stopped by
the city well to rest. And while they were resting, Eliezer began to
think. It was evening and he knew that the women and girls would
be coming to the well to get water for their families. What if one of
THEM was the right girl for Isaac, and how would Eliezer know?

Right then and there, Eliezer asked God for directions.
"Please, God," he said, "when the girls from the village come to
the well to get water, help me choose the right girl for Isaac. I'll
ask her for a drink of water and if she's the right girl, have her give

me a drink and offer to give the camels a drink, too. Help me to find a girl who is kind."

Well that was really asking directions! How could he find a girl who would not only give him a drink—
but give his camels a drink, too?

But Eliezer had no sooner asked that of God, when along came—the most beautiful girl! She was carrying a pitcher on her shoulder. She went to the well and put her pitcher down. Eliezer watched. There was a bucket tied to the well by a rope, and she let the rope down—
      down—
         DOWN—
            until the bucket went
               SPLASH!—and filled with water.
Then she pulled and p-u-l-l-e-d the bucket back up again. She poured the water into her pitcher and started on her way.

Was she the one? Now is the time to find out! Eliezer hurried up to her. "Please," he said, "let me drink a little water from your pitcher."

She gave him the pitcher—and he drank—and handed the pitcher back—and—

"I'll draw water for your camels, also," she said.

Well, when you stop to think that one camel drinks about twenty gallons of water when he's thirsty, and that Eliezer had ten camels with him, and you multiply twenty by ten, you can see that this girl was not just kind, she was FANTASTIC! Eliezer must have felt like a heel watching her draw all that water while he just sat, but he had to find out.

He watched her while she drew water—and more water—and MORE water—for the camels. She was the one! When she had finally finished, he got up and thanked her and then he gave her some beautiful rings and bracelets.

"Whose daughter are you?" he asked. "Is there room for us to stay in your father's house?"

Well, Eliezer was certainly getting NERVIER and NERVIER, but he had to find out. And he did.

She told him her name was Rebekah and there was LOTS of room for them in her father's house.

And when Eliezer went to her father's house and told her father and mother what he had done and how he had found out that God had chosen Rebekah to be Isaac's wife—they let her go back with him!

And that's how it happened that, when Eliezer went back to Abraham, he had a wife for Isaac. Not just ANY wife. But the RIGHT wife. She was extra kind. God had certainly given Eliezer the right directions!

Tracy and Mike Talk It Over

Mike: Wow! Imagine Rebekah drawing all that water. Nobody even asked her to. She didn't have to do that.

Tracy: Well, she was a girl, and girls are always kind.

Mike: Har-de-har-har-har. That's what YOU think!

Tracy: I was only fooling. Some kids are kind and some aren't and it doesn't matter if you're a boy or a girl. Can you think of times when we can be EXTRA kind?

Mike: Sure. You could draw two hundred gallons of water from a well.

Tracy: Come on, Mike, be serious.

Mike: Well, my grandpa lost his glasses one day and he asked me to help him find them, and I found them, but his room was a mess. So I straightened up the papers on his desk and I picked some scrap paper off the floor and put it in the wastebasket for him. He tries to hit the basket from five feet, and he can't even hit it from two feet. He's a bum shot.

Tracy: I could help my mom set the table more often, or dry the dishes, and instead of leaving them on the kitchen counter I could even put them away.

Mike: There must be lots of things we can think of where we can be kind and do extra things for people.

Tracy: I just thought of something. Eliezer asked God for directions because he had a very important job to do. Are we supposed to ask God's directions even if what we have to do isn't very important?

Mike: My mom says that God is interested in everything we do—the big things and the little things.

Tracy: Boy, we have a lot of things to think about. We have to think about asking God for directions and thinking up ways to be extra kind.

Have your puppets take it from here.
(Suggest ways to be extra kind, like doing extra chores, running errands, etc. This should be an easy one.)

A Bible Verse to Learn

Even a child is known by his actions, by whether his conduct is pure and right. Proverbs 20:11

Talk to God

Thank God that when we are extra kind to other people, it makes Him happy, too. Thank Him that you can ask directions when you have to make up your mind about something—and if there are any special directions you need to know, ask Him right now.

Can You Find This Story in the Bible?

Find Genesis 24:1-67.

The Man
Who Ran
Away

Well Isaac and Rebekah got married, and God was good to them. He gave them—not ONE baby—but TWO of them! They were twins—and their names were Esau and Jacob.

God was good to Esau and Jacob, too. They had a good father and mother. They had lots of things to do. They could play together and make bows and arrows and hunt.

But one thing was wrong.

They couldn't get along together. They quarreled and pushed and kicked.

When they grew up to be men, God was still good to them. They had everything—sheep and cattle and gold and silver. They could work together and make bows and arrows and hunt.

But the same thing was still wrong.

They couldn't get along together. They quarreled and lied and cheated.

One day, Jacob cheated his brother Esau—and Esau was SO angry that Jacob was afraid. His mother, Rebekah, was afraid, too. "You'd better go away before Esau hurts you," she told Jacob. "Go back to my country and stay with my brother Laban for awhile." And that's how it happened that Jacob ran away.

He said good-bye to his mother and father. But he didn't say good-bye to Esau. He was afraid of Esau.

Animals still graze in the rocky area around Bethel. It was at Bethel that Jacob used a stone as a pillow. In a dream God promised Jacob that He would be with him and take care of him. When Jacob woke up, he took his stone pillow and set it up for an altar and thanked God for His promise. (Photo © Stacey Martin)

Jacob ran away without camels. Without servants. Without friends. He hurried through the stony paths of the hill country. He walked across the fields of the flat country. And he sneaked through the mountain passes. And wondered every minute if Esau was following!

As the sun went down, every shadow looked like Esau. And when it got dark, every noise sounded like Esau. Jacob curled up on the ground and put his head on a stone. He felt as if NOBODY cared what happened to him. "Nobody is with me," he thought. And then he fell asleep. He was sleeping soundly,

when—

suddenly—

there was a great big ladder, right before Jacob's eyes! It started at the ground and reached all the way up to the sky. And there were angels going up and coming down. And he heard the voice of God saying, "I am with you—and I will watch over you wherever you go."

It was a dream! Why, Jacob wasn't alone—GOD was with him!

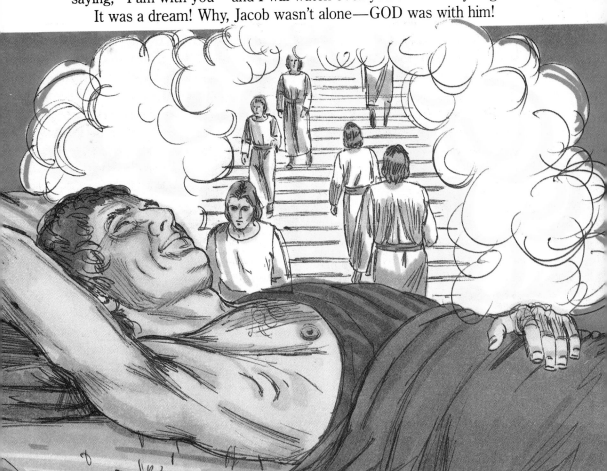

Then suddenly the ladder was gone—
and the angels were gone—
and God's voice was gone—
and Jacob awoke.

But he didn't feel alone any more. And he didn't feel afraid any more. He took the stone he had used for a pillow, and set it up for an altar, and thanked God for watching over him. And he started on his way again—

Without camels. Without servants. Without friends.

But God was with him. And he knew he'd be all right. He knew he'd get to his Uncle Laban's house safely.

And he did!

Tracy and Mike Talk It Over

Mike: Boy, Jacob sure disobeyed God.

Tracy: He quarreled with his brother Esau.

Mike: And he lied and cheated. I'm surprised that God even spoke to him at all.

Tracy: But God did. He even promised to watch over him!

Mike: How do you figure that out?

Tracy: Maybe it's because God is kind even when we aren't. And besides I think God knew Jacob was scared. And that he was sorry.

Have your puppets take it from here.

A Bible Verse to Learn

God says, *I am with you and will watch over you wherever you go.* Genesis 28:15

Talk to God

Thank God that He is still with you even when you disobey. Ask Him to help you obey Him and not to try to find excuses to **disobey.**

Can You Find This Story in the Bible?

Find Genesis 27:41-46; 28:1-22; 29:1-13.

Two Brothers in Trouble

Jacob went to live with his Uncle Laban, and got married and started a cattle business of his own. And then—his family grew and grew until he had eleven children and many servants. And his business grew until he had cattle and sheep by the thousands.

The weeks went by and the months went by, until TWENTY YEARS had gone by—and Jacob had almost everything in the world he wanted.

Except for one thing.

Jacob wanted to go back home. He thought about it and thought about it. And then—one day God told him he COULD go back to his own country again—and God said, "I will be with you."

A trip back home! Just imagine that!

Jacob and his family and servants packed their things and started out—with camels and donkeys and sheep and cattle and just about everything they could carry. What a cloud of dust they made as they traveled across the desert! Jacob thought of his mother and father and Esau—

ESAU!

Would Esau still want to kill him? Jacob became more afraid by the minute.

He sent some servants ahead with a message to his brother Esau that he was on the way. It was a very polite message, and

Jacob waited anxiously for his servants to bring the answer. And when the answer came—

It wasn't polite—

It wasn't IMpolite—

It was FRIGHTENING!

It said that Esau was coming to meet Jacob—with 400 men! What did it mean? Jacob didn't know. But it was time for him to get busy.

First he divided his family and servants and cattle into two groups, so if Esau killed one group there would still be some left. Then he knelt down and asked God to help him. And then he sent servants ahead with a gift for Esau. A BIG gift. Hundreds of goats and sheep and camels and cows and donkeys.

And then both groups traveled on.

While they traveled, Jacob thought, "Esau—Esau—Esau—." And the clop-clop of the camels' feet seemed to say, "Eee—sau, Eee—sau, Eee—sau"—until, suddenly

there off in the distance—

Esau was coming!

Esau came closer and closer and CLOSER—

And Jacob could stand it no longer. He ran ahead of his servants and his cattle and his family. He ran toward Esau. Then he bowed to the ground. And he ran and he bowed and he ran and he bowed, until he had bowed seven times. And Esau ran toward Jacob—and he put his arms around Jacob's neck—and kissed him!

It was over—the quarreling and hating and cheating. Esau forgave his brother and they made up, right then and there. And then they all went back home together.

Now Jacob could be COMPLETELY happy. He had his family—he was going home—and his brother Esau had forgiven him. That was something to thank God for.

And Jacob did!

Tracy and Mike Talk It Over

Mike: Do you think Jacob was a coward?

Tracy: No. I think it was okay for him to be afraid.

Mike: Me, too. I know **I'd** be afraid if Esau was coming at ME.

Tracy: What if somebody had a right to be angry with you—would you be afraid to face him and ask him to forgive you?

Mike: Or what if somebody did something mean to you—would you forgive him?

Have your puppets take it from here.

A Bible Verse to Learn

Be kind and loving to each other. Forgive each other just as God forgave you in Christ. Ephesians 4:32, *ICB*

Talk to God

Thank God that He is with you when you are afraid. Ask Him to help you to forgive when someone is mean to you and then wants to make up. And if **you** have been mean—ask His forgiveness—and ask Him to help you make up. Don't ever stay angry!

Can You Find This Story in the Bible?

Find Genesis 31:3-5; 32:1-32; 33:1-20.

The Gift that Caused Trouble

Now ordinarily a gift is a very jolly thing. You open it and you are jolly and you thank the one who gave it to you and he is jolly and you show it to your friends and they are jolly and there you have it; nothing but fun and happiness. Everybody knows that. But the gift in this story was NOT ordinary. This gift brought nothing but trouble—to a boy named Joseph.

Joseph lived way back in Bible times, and he was the happiest, bubbliest boy you could ever imagine. He was tall and strong, and he could leap over a wall or scramble through the bushes faster than the best of them. He had ten BIG brothers and one baby brother, and when they all sat around the breakfast table and passed the barley cakes and honey, there was always plenty of excitement.

Their father Jacob was very rich, and the sheep and goats and cattle and donkeys he owned were more than you could count. Joseph helped his father and brothers watch the sheep and cattle. He hunted, and he rode the donkeys and camels—and stopped sometimes to tickle his baby brother's feet. And everything was fine, until that gift came along.

When Jacob called Joseph to his tent to give him the gift,

58

Joseph came running as if he had springs in his feet.

"What is it, Father?" he asked. Jacob held out the gift, took it by the top and shook out its beautiful colors.

It was a COAT. The most beautiful coat Joseph had ever seen!

"Is it MINE, Father?" he cried. Jacob nodded yes. His eyes were twinkling. And he held out the coat for Joseph to slip into.

Joseph felt the soft, fine cloth slither over his shoulders.

He looked down at the bright colors in amazement.

The coat went nearly to his ankles! And it had long sleeves! Ordinarily coats were shorter and had short sleeves. Clearly, this was a most extraordinary gift!

"It's the most beautiful coat I've ever seen, Father! Why, only favorite sons wear coats like this!" And he thanked his father and scampered off to show his brothers the gift.

But his brothers didn't say it was beautiful. They scowled—hrummmmf—and they mumbled—mumblmumblmumbl—and scuffed the ground with their feet. They were angry. And they were jealous. Joseph went back to the tent, the springs gone from his feet.

Yes—a gift is supposed to bring happiness. But this one brought nothing but trouble. Trouble to a boy named Joseph and to his whole family. Because Joseph's brothers were jealous.

But Joseph knew that God was watching over him and that God would take care of him. And God did.

Tracy and Mike Talk It Over

Tracy: Do you think Joseph's brothers had a right to be jealous?

Mike: Sure they did. That was a very special coat. It meant that Joseph was the favorite son. Well, maybe they didn't have a right to be jealous, but they had a REASON.

Tracy: Have you ever been jealous?

Mike: Sure. A kid on my block got a new skateboard and I sure was jealous of him. I got one later, but he was way ahead of me. He could skate a lot better than I could.

Tracy: How do you feel when you get jealous?

Mike: I get a little twinge right down through the middle of me. It's sort of like a pin-n-n-g!

Tracy: I get prickles in the back of my neck and I get very sad inside and sort of HEAVY. I don't like it when I feel that way.

Mike: Well, my dad says God doesn't like it when we feel that way either.

Tracy: What does God want us to do?

Mike: He wants us to LOVE the person we're jealous of.

Tracy: Oh-OOOOOOH! That's hard to do.

Mike: You BET it's hard to do. Can you think of anybody you're jealous of right now?

Tracy: I can, but I don't want to talk about it.

Mike: Well, sometimes just talking to God about it makes it go away. You might as well tell Him about it 'cause He knows about it anyway.

Let your puppets take it from there.

Encourage them to talk about their feelings. Help them to think of ways in which they can show love instead of jealousy.

A Bible Verse to Learn

Jesus said, *This is my command: Love each other.* John 15:17

Talk to God

Thank God for all the things you DO have, and ask Him to forgive you if you are feeling jealous and to take away the pings and prickles and the heavy sadness too. And don't let jealousy get you down. Remember, EVERYBODY is jealous of SOMEBODY—SOMETIMES.

Can You Find This Story in the Bible?

Find Genesis 37:1-4.

The Dreams that Caused Trouble

Joseph had everything that a boy could want. But there was one thing wrong. His brothers were jealous. They were jealous because their father Jacob gave Joseph a beautiful coat. And, as if that weren't enough, two OTHER things happened to make them jealous! Two dreams! And Joseph dreamed them.

The first dream was a strange one. Joseph probably told his brothers about it at breakfast.

"Know what?" said Joseph. "I had the most amazing dream last night." And he reached for the barley cakes. "In my dream, we were all tying grain up in bundles. And MY bundle stood up straight. But YOUR bundles—" He asked for the honey. His brothers watched him.

"And our bundles? What did our bundles do?" they asked. Joseph poured his honey on his barley cakes. "YOUR bundles—" he said, "bowed down to MY bundle."

Nobody said anything for a minute. Then they all began to talk at once.

"Do you think you are going to be a KING?" they asked. "Do you think you will rule over US?" Joseph shrugged his shoulders and helped himself to more honey. But the brothers were angry.

THAT dream was bad enough, but when the SECOND dream
came along—Well!

"I had another dream," said Joseph. "This time it was stars."

They all stopped to listen.

Stars!

"Eleven of them," said Joseph. "And that's not all. The sun and
the moon bowed down to me, too!"

THIS was too much! Even Jacob thought this was too much.
"Come now, my son," he said. "If the eleven stars are supposed to
be your brothers—are you trying to tell us that the sun and the
moon were your father and mother? Do you think your father and
mother are going to bow down to you, too?"

"WE'LL never bow down to you!" said his brothers. "Not if we
can help it!" They were very angry.

But Jacob thought and thought about it. DID God have
something special planned for Joseph's life? What if that dream
came TRUE?

Yes, Joseph had everything a boy could want. What if some day
he DID become a big, important ruler? There were lots of exciting
things ahead. And lots of trouble, too! But God was still watching
over Joseph.

Tracy and Mike Talk It Over

Tracy: Mike, do you have a sneaking suspicion that Joseph was a bit of a show-off?

Mike: Well, he sure acted pretty cocky to me.

Tracy: Suppose you knew something nobody else knew? Or that you could do something better than any of the other kids could. Like read better or maybe play the piano. Would you brag about it?

Mike: Well, I don't know. Maybe I might. I'm the best batter in Little League baseball. I never bragged about it, but maybe I FEEL cocky inside.

Tracy: Well, I can read better than anybody my age. I could read lots of words when I was four years old. And I knew the whole alphabet. I never thought about it, but maybe I've felt cocky sometimes—inside.

Let your puppets take it from there.

Explain to them that God gives each of us different gifts. Ask them to tell about what special gifts they think God has given them. And explain to them that they should just be grateful to God instead of being cocky.

A Bible Verse to Learn

(Jesus said), *Love your neighbor as yourself.* Matthew 22:39

Talk to God

Thank God for all the special things He has given you and done for you. Maybe He has given you the gift of being friendly to people. That's a gift, too! Just thank Him for any gift He has given to you. Ask Him to help you never, never to be cocky about it. When you feel jealous of someone, ask God to help you love that person instead of being jealous.

Can You Find This Story in the Bible?

Find Genesis 37:5-11.

The Errand that Ended in Trouble

Joseph's brothers hated him.

"Dreamer!" they said, whenever he walked past.

"Good-bye, Dreamer!" they laughed when they went off to another part of the country to find new pastures for the sheep and cattle.

After they were gone, Joseph didn't have any more dreams. And as the weeks went by, he forgot about trouble.

And then, one day, Jacob gave Joseph a very important errand to do.

"My son," said Jacob, "I want you to find your brothers and bring me back news that they are safe."

Go find his brothers! Why they were in Shechem—at least 60 miles away! It would mean walking all day and sleeping out at night—

"Yes SIR!" said Joseph as he started to get ready. "I'll be careful, Father," he said as he strapped his lunch on his back and kissed his father good-bye. And he started out on the biggest job his father had ever given him to do.

It was dangerous and exciting, traveling the country alone. But when he got to Shechem and found out that his brothers had gone on to Dothan, it seemed more dangerous and less exciting. Dothan was another twenty miles away! What to do? Go on or go back? Joseph decided to go on.

Joseph must have traveled through this valley when he went from Shechem to Dothan to find his brothers. Shepherds still lead their sheep through this area today. (Photo © Stacey Martin)

The last twenty miles were hard going. Joseph was glad when he saw his brothers in the distance. "Now—at last," he thought, "the danger is over."

But the danger was just BEGINNING.

When his brothers saw him coming, they said, "Look! Here comes the 'dreamer.'" They saw the bright colors of his coat in the distance. They remembered the dreams. And they were angry all over again.

"Let's kill him!" they said. "Let's throw him into a pit and say he was killed by a wild beast."

But the oldest brother, Reuben, knew that was wrong.

"No—let's just throw him into a pit alive and leave him there to die," he said. But he was thinking, "I'll come back and save Joseph after my other brothers have gone."

Poor Joseph didn't know any of this when he ran up to his brothers and said, "Father sent—"

And THEN—

They grabbed him. They pulled off his coat. They dragged him to the pit. And—hup!—pushed him in!

"Please—!" he called. But nobody answered. Had they gone off to leave him die?

Joseph thought the end had come. And Reuben thought he would come back and save Joseph.

But they were BOTH wrong!

God had planned something ELSE—something neither of them had dreamed of! Something that changed Joseph's whole life!

It happened while Reuben was gone to look for another place to take their sheep. And while the brothers were eating their lunch. Joseph heard them munching and grumbling softly to themselves. And then—and then—

He heard them scrambling to their feet.

"What's that, way off there? Do you see it?" they cried.

"It's a caravan of merchants!"

"They're on their way to Egypt to sell their goods!"

Joseph stood up in the pit and strained his ears to listen. And the next thing he heard made him sit right back down again. His knees were like jelly.

"Why not sell Joseph?"

Had he heard them right?

"Yes! Sell him to the merchants. Then we won't have to kill him. And we'll never have to see this 'dreamer' again."

He HAD heard them right for the next thing Joseph knew, some of his brothers were shouting to the merchants to stop. And some of them were on their bellies alongside the pit, and reaching down to drag him back up out of it.

And the next thing he knew, the merchants were looking him over and saying, "hmmmmmm. He looks pretty good. We'll give you twenty pieces of silver for him."

And the NEXT thing he knew, he was marching off with the caravan. His brothers had sold him like a loaf of bread!

He kept looking back at them as they got smaller and smaller and smaller until they were just little specks. And he knew that there was nothing left to prove that he had ever been there with his brothers.

Except his beautiful coat, all crumpled up on the ground.

Tracy and Mike Talk It Over

Mike: Wow! What would you do if you were in a spot like that?

Tracy: Well, I don't suppose I'd ever be in a spot like that.

Mike: Suppose you were lost somewhere and you didn't know which way to turn, or you didn't know where to go?

Tracy: Or suppose you were on a picnic with your parents and maybe you wandered off and got lost or something. And you yelled and yelled—and nobody heard you. What would you do?

Mike: Well, in the first place I wouldn't wander off. I would never get in a strange car or I would never go off with a stranger. My parents taught me this.

Tracy: But, would you think about God then? Would you know that He was watching over you?

Mike: Well, if I ever got in a spot like that, I would sure know that God was watching over me, and I would call out to Him, you bet.

Tracy: Well, if you ever got in a spot like that, you'd BETTER call on God.

Let your puppets take it from here.

Help them talk about ways to avoid getting into trouble. Help them think about remembering their phone numbers and addresses and remembering that God is always watching over them.

A Bible Verse to Learn

God says, *Call to me and I will answer you.* Jeremiah 33:3

Talk to God

Thank God for always watching over you. Ask Him to help you to remember all the things you should do to keep from getting into trouble. And thank Him for your parents who love you, and thank Him that they care about you and that they are always praying to God to keep you safe.

Can You Find This Story in the Bible?

Find Genesis 37:12-30.

The Lie
that Broke
Jacob's Heart

Joseph was on his way to Egypt, and his brothers were left behind with his beautiful coat. So far, so good, they thought. But they knew their troubles weren't over; they still had to face Reuben when he came back. They wondered what he would say. They did not have to wait long to find out.

When Reuben came back and discovered that Joseph was gone, he was HORRIFIED. He tore his clothes and cried out to his brothers—"Joseph is GONE! How can I face Father? What can I DO?"

There was only one thing they could think of to do. They took Joseph's coat. And they dipped it in goat's blood. And they tore it. And they rolled it in the sand.

"We'll tell our father we found Joseph's coat," they said, "and he will think a wild animal killed Joseph."

And that's what they did.

"Well," they thought, "that's the end of Joseph!"

A few days later they started back home to their father Jacob. When they got there, sure enough, the first thing he asked was "Where's Joseph?"

"Joseph?" they said. "We don't know. We haven't seen him."

Jacob was frightened. "Why, I sent him to look for you!" Where is he?"

Then the brothers took out the coat, all torn and dirty. They pretended to be worried as they handed it to Jacob.

"We found this coat," they said.

"Do you know if this is Joseph's coat?"

With trembling hands, Jacob took the coat. He looked at its beautiful colors, all dirty. And he began to cry.

"It's Joseph's coat," he cried. "It's my son's beautiful coat. He has been killed by wild animals!"

"My son is dead!" he moaned. And he went weeping into his tent.

The brothers looked at each other. "The lie has worked," they thought. "That is the end of Joseph."

But it wasn't the end—it was a new beginning!

Tracy and Mike Talk It Over

Mike: Boy, was that ever a BIG LIE Joseph's brothers told their father. Would you ever tell a lie like that?

Tracy: Well, no, I would never tell a lie like that. But I HAVE told lies, sometimes.

Mike: Well, so have I, but I talked to my dad about it, and do you know what he told me? The worst part of telling a lie—is to try to cover it up afterward.

Tracy: Yeah—That makes the lie even WORSE—when you try to cover it up afterward.

Mike: I did that once. I took my brother's bike, only he didn't know about it. And I got a big dent in it. I sneaked it back into the garage and then I tried to cover it up. I lied; I said I didn't take it. But I did. I tried to cover up my lie, but it didn't work.

Tracy: Why didn't it work? What happened?

Mike: Well, I finally had to confess that I had taken it. And my dad took me up to my bedroom and we had a lonnng talk. And he told me that it was bad enough that I took the bike—but it was even WORSE to try to cover it up. Did you ever lie, Tracy?

Tracy: Well, yes. One time I was sent to the store to buy some candy for everybody, and I bought a whole bunch of peanut squares and on the way home I began to nibble off the edges of them, and then they weren't squares anymore, they were oblong, so I nibbled off the ends to make them squares again. And by the time I got home they were so small, that everybody knew that I'd been nibbling on them and I lied to try to cover it up. I just told them that they were selling the squares smaller these days. It didn't work. Everybody knew I was lying, and my mother took me aside and told me that it wasn't so bad that I'd nibbled off the peanut squares, but it was VERY BAD that I had lied to try to cover the truth. It's really dumb to do something like that.

Mike: Yes—it's bad enough to lie, but it's even worse to try to cover it up.

Tracy: Yes, I guess it's best not to lie in the first place.

Let your puppets take it from here.

Encourage them to tell when they have told a lie and how dumb it is to try to cover it up.

A Bible Verse to Learn

Do not lie to each other. Colossians 3:9

Talk to God

Thank God for teaching you how bad it is to lie—and to cover up wrongdoing with lies. Ask Him to forgive you for every time you've ever told a lie. Thank Him that He forgives you.

Can You Find This Story in the Bible?

Find Genesis 37:31-35.

The Dreams that Came True

Poor Joseph's father! He cried for MONTHS. For he thought his son was dead. But the brothers kept whispering to each other, "The lie has worked. That's the end of Joseph."

But it wasn't the end. For at that very moment Joseph was being taken to Egypt. Egypt—with houses and temples instead of tents! And streets and shops and crowds of people! And a slave market!

Ah yes, the slave market. That's where he was taken. And that's where he was SOLD. He was sold as a slave, to a man named Potiphar. But God was still watching over Joseph. For Potiphar was an important man. In fact, Potiphar was an officer of the king! And what happened?

Well, Joseph worked hard, and Potiphar was kind to him. Joseph worked harder still, and Potiphar began to trust him. Joseph worked harder than EVER—and finally—Potiphar made him master over all the other slaves in his house!

And then—

And THEN—something happened to spoil it all!

It was another lie! This time it was Potiphar's WIFE who told the lie. She told Potiphar that Joseph had done something very wicked. And Potiphar believed her and put Joseph in—of all places—PRISON!

In Egypt today we can still see great temples like those Joseph saw in Bible times. Notice how huge this temple at Karnak was. (Photo © Joyce Thimsen)

This was REAL trouble. But Joseph had been in trouble before, and by this time he knew that the best thing to do in trouble was to behave himself. He worked hard, and the jailer was kind to him. He worked harder still, and the jailer began to trust him. He worked harder than EVER—

Joseph wondered, as the months went by, if he would ever get out of prison. He knew they wouldn't let him out for no reason at all. Something SPECIAL would have to happen. And something did. It was another dream.

This time it wasn't Joseph who had the dream. It was another prisoner. He was the butler to Pharaoh, the great king of Egypt, and he had such a strange dream that he told Joseph about it.

"I dreamed," he said, "that there was a vine in front of me. It had three branches. First the vine had buds on it, and then flowers—and then grapes! I squeezed the grape juice into a cup and gave it to Pharaoh. What does this dream mean?"

"It means," said Joseph, "that in three days you will be out of prison and back to your job as butler in the palace."

And it happened—just as Joseph said it would! Three days later, Pharaoh had a birthday party and sent for his butler to come back to the palace!

"Now," said Joseph, as the butler left, "will you do me a favor? Will you tell the king I have done no wrong, and ask him to get me out of this prison?"

The butler promised and went happily on his way.

The days went by, and Joseph waited. He waited and waited—until TWO WHOLE YEARS went by!

And then a strange thing happened. It was another dream.

This time it was Pharaoh, the king of Egypt, who had the dream. And none of Pharaoh's wise men could tell what it meant. Then—at last—the butler remembered Joseph. And the dream. And his promise! Right then and there he told the Pharaoh that Joseph could tell him what his dream meant. "Send for him," cried the Pharaoh, "at once!" And that's how it happened that one minute Joseph was in prison and the NEXT thing he knew, he was standing before the king!

"I dreamed," the king told Joseph, "that I saw seven fat cows and seven thin cows come out of the river. And right before my eyes, the thin cows ate up the fat cows.

"Then I went back to sleep and dreamed another dream. I saw seven fat ears of corn growing on one stalk. Then seven bad ears of corn came up. And right before my eyes, the seven bad ears ate up the good ears. What does it mean?"

"It means," said Joseph, "that for seven years there will be lots to eat in the land. Then—for seven years nothing will grow. There won't be any grain. And the people won't have any food!"

Pharaoh was worried. "What shall we do, Joseph?" he asked.

"Well," said Joseph, "the first seven years you'll have more than you need. God wants you to save what's left over and store it in big barns. Then when the grain doesn't grow you'll have enough food. You must find a very wise man to see that the food is saved."

Pharaoh thought a minute. Then he looked at Joseph. "You," he said. "You are JUST the man."

Pharaoh took off his ring. He put it on Joseph's finger. And he said, "I hereby make you the man in charge of all Egypt."

Just like that. In a moment, Joseph was changed from a poor prisoner to the head man in all Egypt, next to the king!

He traveled all over Egypt, making the people build big barns and store food. He lived in a palace. And nobody in Egypt was more powerful than Joseph, except the king. At last things were going well with Joseph.

Yes, it took a long time. But God was certainly watching over Joseph, every step of the way.

Tracy and Mike Talk It Over

Mike: Wow! Just think of all the things that happened to Joseph.

Tracy: Yes—the people who didn't keep their promises and the people who lied about him.

Mike: Did you ever have people lie about you and get you into trouble?

Tracy: Well, I can't think of anything this minute, but I'll bet if I thought about it, I could. Sure people have lied about me.

Mike: And what did you do about it?

Tracy: Well, I felt AWFUL.

Mike: Did you get angry? Did you fight back?

Tracy: I probably got angry. And maybe I fought back sometimes. But I probably shouldn't have fought back. I should have remembered that God was watching over me and that He would make it all right.

Mike: Well, what if somebody lied about you and said you cheated on a test or something, and you didn't cheat at all—maybe he cheated. Maybe he copied your paper. What would you do?

Tracy: That's a tough one. I don't know what I'd do. I'll have to think about it.

Let your puppets take it from here.

Encourage them to remember when somebody has lied about them and what they did about it.

A Bible Verse to Learn

Do not be afraid or discouraged, for the LORD God, My God, is with you. 1 Chronicles 28:20

Talk to God

Thank God that He cares about you and that whatever happens to you—that God knows all about it.

Can You Find This Story in the Bible?

Find Genesis 39:1-23; 40:1-23; 41:1-57.

The Journey with Nine Surprises

God had thought of everything. Joseph was ruler over all Egypt, next to the king. For seven years, he made the people store food in big barns. And then the Pharaoh's dream began to come true.

Famine!

Just as Joseph had said, the grain didn't grow—and there wasn't any food anywhere—except in the big barns. People came from all over the country to buy food. They came from other countries, too, for the famine was all over the land.

And then, one day—another dream began to come true. It was Joseph's own dream—the one he'd had so many years before! And this is how it happened.

One day Joseph was selling grain from one of the big barns. The people were streaming in from everywhere. Joseph watched them as they bought their food and hurried on their way. And then—

suddenly—

his heart almost stopped beating. Out of the crowds came ten shepherds who looked as if they had traveled a long way. They looked familiar.

They came closer—and Joseph thought, "Could they be?"
They knelt down before him and bowed their heads to the
ground—and Joseph thought, "They ARE. They are my brothers!"
And they WERE his brothers—all there except his youngest
brother, Benjamin.

Joseph thought of his dream, which was coming true right
before his eyes. His brothers were bowing down to him, just as the
eleven bundles of grain and the eleven stars had, in his dreams!

Eleven.

But there were only ten brothers there. Where was Benjamin?
And where was his father? Joseph had to find out without letting
his brothers know who he was.

"Who are you?" he said. "Where do you come from?"

"We are from Canaan," they said, bowing lower than ever.

"You are spies!" cried Joseph, pretending to be angry. And he
asked them all sorts of questions with a scowling face but he didn't
tell them who he was. And they quaked and trembled as they
answered. And he found out—

Benjamin was alive.

His father was alive.

And none of them had any food.

Well, for the next few days, those poor brothers didn't know
whether they were coming or GOING. First Joseph told them he
would send one of them home to get their brother Benjamin while
the rest of them waited in Egypt. Then he put them all in prison!
THEN—at the end of three days, he told them they could ALL go
home but Simeon. By this time they were thoroughly confused and
very frightened.

"Leave Simeon here," he said. "The rest of you go home and
take some food, but bring your youngest brother back. Then I'll
know if you're telling the truth."

"This is what we deserve," said the brothers, "for selling poor
Joseph to be a slave and for telling our father a lie." They spoke in
their own language. They didn't think the great Egyptian ruler
could understand them.

But the great Egyptian ruler DID understand them. For he was
their own brother Joseph.

But they did not know it when they started their journey back
home to their father.

Their donkeys were loaded up to their long ears with sacks of grain. As the brothers traveled along, they were half-happy and half-frightened because they'd had to leave Simeon behind in prison. They wondered how they were going to tell their father Jacob.

When night came and the desert pulled long shadows up over its toes to get ready for bed, the brothers stopped to rest. And that's when they found the first surprise. One of them opened a sack of grain to feed the donkeys—and stopped and stared. "My moneybag," he said. "It's full of money." He dumped it out and counted it. "I used all my money to pay for the food," he said. "But it's all here. Every bit."

Nobody knew what to say for a minute. Then they all began to talk at once. "The ruler will think you STOLE it," they cried. "What shall we do?"

There was nothing they COULD do. They went to sleep, more frightened than they had ever been in their lives. And in the morning they went on with their journey.

When they got home, their father Jacob knew at once that something was wrong. "Where's Simeon?" he said. And they told him everything. About the ruler of Egypt. And how he thought they were wicked men. And made them leave Simeon in prison. And asked them to bring Benjamin back, so he would know they were telling the truth. And they told Jacob how they had found the money.

"Oh, Simeon!" wailed Jacob. And, "Oh my poor Benjamin! I will not send him to Egypt. He may be killed. See the trouble you have got us in!"

The brothers didn't know what to say. They began to unpack another donkey. And that's when they found the second surprise. Another bag of money! Then they unpacked donkeys so fast their heads were spinning.

Three donkeys—
  four— five— six—
       seven— eight— NINE!

And nine bags of money! Every bit of the money the brothers had taken with them!

"The ruler of Egypt will think we are thieves," they said. "We are really in trouble."

The nine surprises made them very frightened. But they didn't know the ruler of Egypt was Joseph. They didn't know he returned good for evil and gave them surprises as gifts. And they didn't know that—the biggest surprise was yet to come!

Tracy and Mike Talk It Over

Mike: Woooeee! Joseph gave his brothers all their money back! Imagine that! And after they had been so *mean* to him!

Tracy: My dad says that Joseph was returning good for evil. The Bible says we're supposed to do that.

Mike: Can you think of anybody who had been mean to you—and *you* returned good for evil?

Tracy: Well, there was a girl in my class once. And she had been mean to me. She had talked to other kids about me. And she had even told lies about me. And I didn't like her for a long, long time. And then one day the teacher chose me to be traffic monitor. And I had to choose some helpers. And I knew she wanted to be one of them.

Mike: You didn't choose *her*, did you?

Tracy: Well, first I didn't *want* to, but finally I did.

Mike: Was that hard to do?

Tracy: It was hard right up 'till I chose her. But the minute I chose her, I felt good all over. And after that, we were friends again.

Mike: Did she ever tell you she was sorry?

Tracy: No, but I knew she was sorry. And my mom said I did what was right. Besides, maybe that taught her a lesson. Can you think of any time somebody was mean to you? What did *you* do?

Mike: I'm thinking, I'm thinking . . .

Let your puppets take over from here.

You may find there is some "unfinished business" to take care of. Perhaps the puppets can talk about somebody who has been mean to them, and they are still angry about it. If not, you can invent situations and let the puppets talk these situations out and decide what they should do.

A Bible Verse to Learn

Love your enemies, do good to those who hate you. Luke 6:27

Talk to God

Thank God that He has given you a Bible to show you what to do when somebody is mean to you. Ask Him to forgive you if there is somebody in your life who has been mean to you and you are still angry about it. And ask God to show you what to do!

Can You Find This Story in the Bible?

Find Genesis 42:1-38.

The Biggest Surprise of All

Joseph's brothers and their father Jacob had food. But they were sad. Because Simeon was in prison in Egypt. And the Egyptian ruler thought they were thieves.

When it was time to go back for more food, they were sadder still. Because poor Benjamin had to go with them. "You MUST let us take Benjamin," the brothers told Jacob, "or the ruler won't even see us." And poor Jacob had to let Benjamin go.

But when they got back to Egypt, they had MORE surprises waiting for them.

They took Benjamin up to the great ruler, and stood there trembling. And then they had the first surprise. Instead of putting them in prison, the ruler told his servant to take them to his palace for dinner! "Now we ARE in trouble," they thought. "He's going to make us all his slaves."

When they got to the palace, the brothers tried to explain to the ruler's head servant. "We found the money in our sacks," they said. "We didn't steal it."

The servant smiled. "It must have been God who put the money in your sacks," he said. "I received the money for your grain." And before they could get over that surprise, the servant brought Simeon out to them.

It was all so topsy turvey! They all expected to be put IN prison—and instead, Simeon was OUT of prison. And here they all were, safe and sound, and about to have dinner in a palace!

When the great ruler came in, the brothers all bowed down before him.

"Is this your younger brother?" the ruler asked. They told him yes—and they were too frightened to notice that the ruler had tears in his eyes.

The brothers were frightened all through dinner, and frightened right up until the next surprise. The ruler ordered their donkeys packed with grain and said that the brothers could go home! The poor brothers were quite dizzy with surprises by this time.

Early the next morning they started for home, feeling that they'd had the strangest adventure of their lives. But the surprises weren't over yet.

The brothers hadn't gone very far, when the ruler's chief servant hurried after them. "The ruler's silver cup is missing," he cried. "Why have you stolen it?"

The poor brothers said they hadn't stolen anything, but they were frightened. They unloaded their donkeys—and there was the silver cup—in Benjamin's sack! With heavy hearts, they went back to Egypt and bowed again before the great ruler.

"Please don't punish Benjamin," they begged. "Our poor father will die. Keep one of us as your slave, but let Benjamin go!" Imagine! The same men who sold their brother Joseph were willing to do anything to save their brother Benjamin now! And Joseph knew they had learned their lesson. They weren't wicked any more. He was ready to give them the biggest surprise of all!

"Look at me, he said, "I am your brother Joseph."

Well, THAT surprise was almost too great to believe. They just stared.

"I AM," said Joseph. "Don't be afraid of me. And don't be sorry you sold me as a slave. God has made me ruler of Egypt, so that I could provide you with food." And then he hugged Benjamin, right before their eyes, and they knew he was telling the truth.

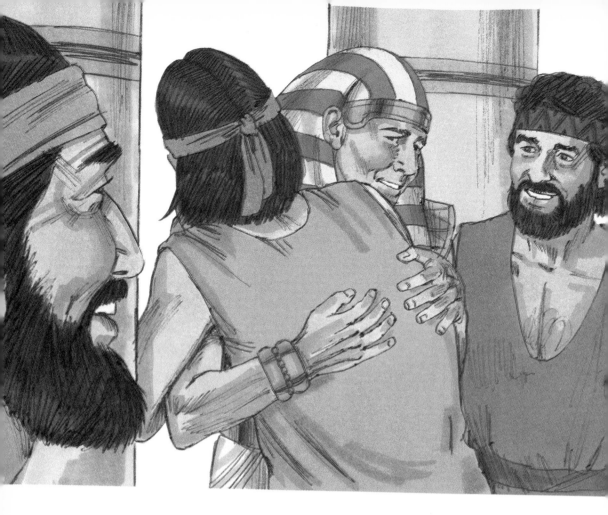

Oh, joy! It was almost too much to believe. Joseph forgave them for the wrong they had done! They all laughed and talked and cried together and thanked God for the biggest surprise of all! They were all together again!

Tracy and Mike Talk It Over

Tracy: Oh, NOW I see why Joseph made them come back and wait and GO back and COME back again. For awhile, I thought he was just being mean, to pay them back for what they had done to him.

Mike: I sorta thought so, too. But he was just testing them. My mom and dad said it was really GOD who was testing them.

Tracy: And then they were even willing to have Joseph keep one of them as a slave if he would only save Benjamin!

Mike: They sure learned their lesson all right.

Tracy: How does it make you feel to know that God is watching you to see how you behave?

Mike: Well, I know God is watching me because He cares about me. But it makes me feel sorta funny to know that PEOPLE are watching me to see what kind of Christian I am. I know a boy who used to be a bully. He picked on kids smaller than he was. And then he realized that people were wondering what kind of Christian HE was. So he stopped. And now he sticks up for little kids when big kids are picking on them.

Tracy: Did you really know somebody like that? Did you really know a bully? Do I know him? Who was he?

Mike: His name was Mike. ME.

Tracy: Oh, wow! You sure are different NOW.

Mike: I learned my lesson, that's for sure. Can you think of other things you need to change, so people will know you really are the Christian you SAY you are?

Let your puppets take over from here.

Help them tell ways THEY can change so that people will know they love Jesus.

A Bible Verse to Learn

Jesus said, *All men will know that you are my disciples if you love one another.* John 13:35

Talk to God

Thank God for always giving you a chance to change. Ask Him to help you remember that when you behave badly, people DO notice what kind of Christian you really are.

Can You Find This Story in the Bible?

Find Genesis 43:1-34; 44:1-32; 45:1-15.

The Best
News of All

Joseph was together with his brothers at last. Oh, joy! That was the best surprise of all. There was only one thing missing. Joseph wanted to see his father Jacob and tell him the good news.

Joseph and his brothers shared their surprise with everybody. And the news traveled fast. When it reached Pharaoh, the king of Egypt, he sent for Joseph. "Tell your brothers to go home and get all their families. And your father. And come back here to LIVE. Give them extra donkeys and food and wagons—everything they need."

Oh, joy! Now the surprise was almost complete!

Joseph told his brothers the good news. And then they all got busy. They got together extra donkeys
　　　　　　　　and food
　　　　　　　　　　and gifts
　　　　　　　　　　　　and wagons—
　　　　　　　　　　　　　　and at last—
the brothers were ready to go.

"Don't get too excited on the way!" said Joseph, as he waved good-bye.

Excited!

The brothers were BURSTING with excitement all the way! They could hardly wait to see their father and make the surprise complete.

When they finally got home, dear old Jacob just stood there staring. There were ALL his sons! Safe and sound! With extra donkeys and wagons—just LOADED!

"Joseph is still alive, Father" the brothers cried, "And he's ruler of Egypt!"

Jacob just stood there, stunned.

"It's true, Father. The ruler we told you about is Joseph. OUR Joseph." And they told him everything that had happened to them—all talking at once. They unloaded the donkeys and wagons and gifts. And finally Jacob had to believe the wonderful news.

"You've said enough," he cried. "I believe you. My Joseph is still alive. And I'm going to see him before I die."

And then they all began to talk about it. They talked about it while the hillside covered itself up with shadows for the night. They talked about it far into the night. And then they DREAMED about it.

For they were all going back to Egypt to make the surprise complete!

Jacob could hardly wait to see his son Joseph. "Joseph, Joseph," he thought, as the families took down the tents and rolled up the rugs and loaded the donkeys and camels for the journey. "My Joseph," he thought, as they gathered the cattle and got ready to leave. "Joseph," his heart sang as he climbed into a wagon and they finally started. "Joseph—Jo-o-o-seph," the wagon wheels seemed to say as they creaked along.

Jacob counted the days. It was so hard to wait! He thought about how OLD he was, and wondered if he'd live to get there safely. He wondered—right up until he had the dream. One night when they stopped to rest, Jacob thanked God for taking care of them and went to sleep.

And that's when it happened.

"Jacob, Jacob!" It was a voice!

Jacob listened hard. "Here I am," he said.

"I am God," said the voice. "Don't be afraid to go to Egypt. I will be with you and keep you safe. And you will see your son Joseph again."

Oh joy!
    Oh wonder!
        God was good!
            Jacob began to count the HOURS.
                "Joseph, J-o-o-o-seph,"
                    creaked the wagon wheels.

When they got near Egypt, Jacob could hardly wait. He sent his son Judah ahead to tell Joseph they were coming. And then he began to count the MINUTES. Would they EVER get there? Jacob strained his eyes to see the first sign of Egypt as he joggled along in his wagon. He watched every cloud of dust, every speck.

And then one cloud of dust became a speck and got bigger and BIGGER. Someone was coming. Was it Judah coming back? Jacob looked HARD. Was it a donkey? No—it was a chariot. A big, beautiful chariot with swift horses and —who?

The chariot came nearer, and Jacob held his breath. The horses stopped by Jacob's wagon, their coats wet and shining from running hard, and sent a swirl of dust up around them.

Judah was in the chariot. And with him was a tall, handsome stranger. With beautiful clothes. And a gold chain around his neck. The ruler of Egypt!

"Joseph!" cried Jacob, hardly daring to believe his eyes. And the big important ruler sprang out of the chariot and took poor old Jacob in his arms. And they both cried together.

"Father, Father," said Joseph, "I could not wait. I had to come to meet you."

What joy there was as they all went on to Egypt together! Joseph introduced them to Pharaoh who gave them the best part of the land to live in. All the surprises were complete at last.

And God had been watching over them all—every minute!

Tracy and Mike Talk It Over

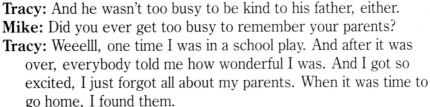

Tracy: Joseph never forgot his father!
Mike: No. Even when Joseph got to be the most powerful man in all Egypt!
Tracy: And he wasn't too busy to be kind to his father, either.
Mike: Did you ever get too busy to remember your parents?
Tracy: Weeelll, one time I was in a school play. And after it was over, everybody told me how wonderful I was. And I got so excited, I just forgot all about my parents. When it was time to go home, I found them.
Mike: Where?

Tracy: I'm ashamed to tell you. I found them waiting for me outside.

Mike: How did that make you feel?

Tracy: I felt AWFUL but it was too late.

Mike: Did they scold you?

Tracy: No. But that made me feel even WORSE. Have you ever forgotten your parents? When they just didn't seem important?

Mike: Well, I can think of sometimes. Sometimes when I made a lot of runs in a Little League baseball game. And everybody crowded around me. And I forgot they had been up there in the stands, cheering me on. I forgot they were even there.

Tracy: When did you remember?

Mike: Later, when they bought me a hot dog.

Tracy: Were they angry? Did they scold you?

Mike: No. They understood how excited I was. They LOVE me. Still, I think you should remember your parents. And introduce them to people. And stuff like that.

Tracy: I guess we should never feel so important that we forget our parents.

Let your puppets take over from here.

Encourage them to think of times they have forgotten their parents. Help them to remember ways in which they should remember their parents, no matter how busy they might be. A hug or a kiss might be a good idea. Parents like to be appreciated.

A Bible Verse to Learn

Honor your father and your mother. Exodus 20:12

Talk to God

Thank God for your parents. And ask Him to help you to remember that your parents like to be appreciated. Not just when you NEED them, but when you're busy, too.

Can You Find This Story in the Bible?

Find Genesis 45:9-28; 46:1-7, 28-34.

A Secret in a Basket

The princess was by the river's edge bathing when she first saw it. It was a basket that had been smeared with tar to keep it from leaking and it was bobbing up and down in the water, kept in one spot by the tall bullrushes that were growing all around it. Whatever could be in it?

She sent one of her maidens for it and waited eagerly for it to be brought to her. When it was set down at last, they all gathered around it. What ever could be inside? A treasure? A secret of some sort? Somebody's lunch?

She took the cover off, slowly, and there was—

A BABY!

It was the most beautiful baby she had ever seen. "Why, it must be one of the Hebrew children," the princess said. "Somebody has put him in the river to save his life. So somebody must be watching over him right now." They all stood up and craned their necks to see, and sure enough, there was a girl standing down by the bullrushes looking up at them and shaking with fear. The princess beckoned for her to come on up. The girl bowed to the princess and her legs got all tangled up like a pretzel, she was so excited.

"Do you want me to get him a nurse?"

And the princess looked at the girl for a moment and said, "All right, go get me a nurse."

The girl ran off without another word and was back in a flash with her mother. The princess looked at them closely. It wasn't too hard to guess that they were both very close to that baby.

"Take care of this baby for me," said the princess, "And I will pay you well. The child will be under my protection so no harm will come to him. When he has grown big enough, you can bring him back to the palace and I will adopt him as my own."

The girl took the basket from the princess and left with the mysterious nurse she had brought to take care of this mysterious baby. For she was the baby's very own sister. And the nurse? The baby's very own mother.

Imagine that!

Oh, what joy there was in that house when the girl brought the baby back to live with his very own family, safe and sound.

But who was this mysterious baby, anyhow, and why did they have to put him in a basket to save his life? And why did they put him on the river's edge right near where the princess came to bathe?

ALL RIGHT, let's untangle this mystery.

The country where all of this took place was the great country of Egypt. And the people there all worshiped idols. But in this country also were a great many Hebrews and they were God's people. And there were thousands of them—thousands and thousands and THOUSANDS of them! And, of course, they all worshiped God. And so, of course, the king hated them. So he made them all his slaves. And they had to work long days in the hot sun, making BRICKS for him to use in all his building projects. And the king was always building something. So there was no end of bricks to be made. They made bricks, and more bricks, and MORE bricks, and when they didn't make enough bricks to suit

This is how the Nile River, in Egypt, looks today. When Moses was a baby, his little basket bed was hidden among the tall bullrushes that grew along this river. As a boy, Moses must have watched boats sail down this river. (Photo © Frances Blankenbaker)

95

him, they were whipped without mercy by their Egyptian overseers. But no matter how badly they were treated, their numbers still kept growing. They had babies and babies and MORE babies. So the king ordered that every baby boy born to the Hebrews had to be KILLED.

So now can you see why the baby's family put him in a basket right in the very spot where the princess was bathing? They HOPED she would find him; and they HOPED she would like him because he was so beautiful; and they HOPED she would take him under her protection. And she DID!

So this beautiful baby lived happily in the home of his parents and his sister, whose name was Miriam, and his brother, whose name was Aaron. They knew that they had him in their home for only a few years, so while he was there they taught him all about God and they made very sure that he knew that he was a HEBREW—one of GOD'S people.

And the princess thought, *I drew this baby out of the*

river, so I'll give him a name that means just that—drawn out of the water.

And that name was—

MOSES.

And Moses turned out to be one of the most important men the world has ever known! Wait and see!

Tracy and Mike Talk It Over

Mike: Boy, Moses sure got pushed around a lot.

Tracy: He sure did. He had a lot of different homes: his parents' home, a basket boat—and later a palace home with the princess who adopted him.

Mike: I wonder how he felt about all that.

Tracy: Yeah—things like that can be pretty upsetting.

Mike: I know a boy a lot of that stuff happened to. First he had his parents and then he had a foster home and then he had another foster home, and he never did get back to see his parents again. How would you feel if all that happened to you?

Tracy: Well, my mom says that God has a plan for your life, no matter how much you get shoved around. And sometimes God lets children know about it, even when they're little kids. Do you believe that? How do you suppose He does it?

Let your puppets take it from here.

Help them think of ways God speaks to them. (In prayer, things they learn from the Bible, etc.)

A Bible Verse to Learn

God says, *I know the plans I have for you.* Jeremiah 29:11

Talk to God

Thank God that He has a plan for your life. And ask Him to show you what it is. Maybe He will give you a hint. Tell Him what you think you'd like to be or what you'd like to do.

Can You Find This Story in the Bible?

Find Exodus 1:1-22; 2:1-10.

The Bush that Didn't Burn

Moses was brought up in the palace and received the finest education and learned all about everything there was to know about the Egyptian ways.

BUT

He was an Egyptian on the outside—and a HEBREW on the INSIDE. And he grieved for his people who were kept in slavery and treated so cruelly. He grieved until he could stand it no longer, and he began to FIGHT with the cruel Egyptian overseers.

WHAM! BAM! OUCH!

When the king heard about it he was FURIOUS, and Moses knew he had to run away, or the king would have him killed. He traveled for miles and miles until he was far enough away from the cruel king to feel safe and there in the desert, he met a shepherd family and settled down to live with them and there he began a brand new life.

And as the years went by, Moses felt less like a prince—and more like a shepherd. And as he watched his sheep under the desert sun, he thought about his own people and his old home. And as he sat under the stars at night, he thought about his real mother and remembered the things she had told him about God.

And then it happened. The most wonderful—and the most FRIGHTENING THING!

Moses was wandering through the wilderness with his sheep when he saw it. It was a bush on fire. Now there was nothing unusual about that—except that THIS bush was on fire but the leaves didn't curl up and fall off, and the branches didn't turn to ashes and drop. Right in the middle of the fire the leaves and branches stayed green and pretty and didn't seem to mind the fire a bit.

Moses just stood and stared. And then he heard a voice.

"Moses . . . Moses!" It was coming from the bush!

"Here I am," said Moses, and he stared some more.

"Take off your sandals," said the voice, "for this is a holy place."

And then Moses knew. He took off his sandals. It was God!

"I know how cruel the king is to the Hebrew people," said God's voice, "I want you to go back and ask the king to let them go. I want YOU to be their leader and lead them out of Egypt."

"I-I-CAN'T," said Moses. "I can't do this great thing alone."

And the voice said, "You won't have to do it alone. I will be with you."

Then the fire was gone. The bush was still there, but the fire was gone and Moses was alone. He was afraid and excited all at the same time. He knew that he had a great and FRIGHTENING job to do, but he knew God would be with him!

Tracy and Mike Talk It Over

Mike: Phew! That's like running away from a roaring lion and then having God ask you to go back and feed him your popcorn.

Tracy: Yes, that surely was a hard thing for God to ask Moses to do.

Mike: Did God ever ask you to do anything hard? I mean hard enough so that you were really scared?

Tracy: Wellll—there is something, but I'm ashamed to tell you what it is because it doesn't SOUND hard. I mean I shouldn't be scared—but I am.

Mike: What is it? Tell me, what is it?

Tracy: It's a girl in my class. She makes fun of me sometimes. She says mean things about me behind my back.

Mike: Well, that's nothing to be SCARED of. She's not going to beat you up or anything like that.

Tracy: No—I keep thinking I ought to tell her about Jesus, and I'm afraid to. She wouldn't beat me up or anything like that. But she might make fun of me.

Mike: But if God tells you to do it, wouldn't you do it anyway, even if she did make fun of you?

Tracy: I'm not so sure. What would you do?

Let your puppets take it from here.

(Parent/teacher: Help your child by asking hypothetical questions: Suppose you came across a group of kids making fun of what the Bible says—what would you say? Suppose someone you knew said he didn't believe in God, what would you say?)

A Bible Verse to Learn

God said, "I will be with you." Exodus 3:12

Talk to God

Thank God that when He asks you to do something that is hard, He promises always to be with you. Ask Him to help you to remember this when things get scary.

Can You Find This Story in the Bible?

Find Exodus 2:11-25; 3:1-22; 4:1-18.

The Journey
that Began
at Midnight

When Moses got to the king, he was no longer frightened. He stood right up to the king, eyeball to eyeball, and said, "Oh, king—God says to let these Hebrews go."

Pharaoh leaned forward on his throne and his voice was like a thunderclap. "And who is GOD that I should let these people go?"

"He is the God of the Hebrews," Moses said. "And He has spoken to me. Let us go."

"The answer is NO!" the king bellowed. "I am the KING and I answer to no one. These people are my slaves. Why do you keep them from doing their work? If they don't have enough to keep them busy, I'll give them MORE!"

And he did.

Then Moses fired his bombshell. "Let us go," he warned, "or God will PUNISH you!"

"I don't believe it," thought Pharaoh, and that was the biggest mistake he ever made in his life.

For there followed a series of punishments so strange and so DREADFUL that there has never been anything like them since in all the world.

First—

The great River Nile that flowed through Egypt and watered all the gardens turned to BLOOD!

Then—

FROGS! God sent frogs—millions of them, they were all over the country. Frogs in the gardens—frogs in the streets—frogs in the houses—frogs in the PALACE—frogs in the Pharaoh's bed—frogs in the BED?!?!!!!?

And then—

FLIES! Horrible stinging flies!

Flies in the houses—flies in the palace—flies in the Pharaoh's bed—flies in the Pharaoh's BED?????!!!!

Then—DISEASE! Then—HAIL! Then—LOCUSTS!

"WAIT!" screamed the king. "Stop it! STOP IT! You may go! Take your women and children, too! But leave your CATTLE behind!"

"No" said Moses.

"Then MY answer is NO!" the king shouted again. He wasn't finished yet.

But neither was God.

"Then tonight about midnight," Moses said quietly, "all the firstborn Egyptian children will die and don't say God didn't warn you."

Well, the king had his warning and he had his chance to change his mind, but he wouldn't listen.

And then—

And THEN—

God said to Moses, "The time has come. You shall lead your people out of Egypt this very night."

And Moses told the people what they were supposed to do.

"Gather all your things," he said. "And prepare a supper. Not any old supper, a SPECIAL SUPPER. Roast lamb and bread and herbs and all cooked in a SPECIAL WAY." And Moses told the people just how to do it—the way God had told him they should. And they did everything Moses told them to do.

And they waited—

Midnight! Then suddenly a cry went up through the air. The firstborn child in every Egyptian family was dead!

And the king sent for Moses. "Go!" he cried.
"ALL of you go, go, GO!
Get out of Egypt and
never come BACK!
And they did. They tumbled out of their houses—
fathers and mothers and children
and grandfathers and grandmothers and
uncles and aunts and cousins.
With goats and sheep and wagons
and carts and donkeys
and bundles—
thousands of them—
thousands and THOUSANDS of them!

Where were they going? And how would they know?

Did Moses know? The people wondered as they marched along.

And then they stopped in their tracks. There ahead of them was a great big cloud—not like any other cloud they had ever seen. "It's God," they cried. "It's God showing us which way to go." And it was.

They followed the cloud all day, and at night when they couldn't see it—but wait! They COULD see it, because it changed into a pillar of fire, lighting up the night. On and on they went until—

What was that? Rumbling? Rumbling of chariot wheels! The king had changed his mind. The Egyptians were coming after them.

And what was THIS?!? Oh, NO! Right in front of them was the Red Sea. There was no place to run!

"Lift up your rod, Moses," God said. "And stretch it out over the sea." Moses did, and all the people watched, holding their breath. Then—WISHHHHH—the wind began to blow. It blew and BLEW and the waters began to pile up and UP, until they divided into two great WALLS of water with a path right through the middle of the sea. There WAS a place to run after all. And run they did. They scrambled and scurried and drove their sheep and cattle ahead and pulled their carts and wagons right through the middle of the sea until they were safe on the other side. And then they looked back.

The Egyptians were coming—down to the edge of the water and through the path, through the sea—right after them!

Moses acted quickly, and as soon as all the Hebrew people were safely across, he stretched out his rod again—and with a mighty ROAR the waters came tumbling, swirling, foaming, back again to cover the path—and the Egyptians disappeared into the sea!

And the cloud? Why, it had scooted right over their heads and gone in front of them—and was waiting there when they all got across.

It was all over. The Hebrew people were safe again. Safe from the Egyptians. And the wicked Pharaoh. They gathered on the shore and thanked God.

Tracy and Mike Talk It Over

Mike: Boy, that's the most exciting story I ever heard. Just think of all the things that God did to make Pharaoh let Moses and his people go!

Tracy: Yeah! And look at all the things He did to help them escape when the Pharaoh was chasing them!

Mike: But He doesn't do things like that for us today.

Tracy: How do you know He doesn't? Maybe He doesn't do the SAME things, but He does other things just as wonderful.

Mike: Name one. Name just one. Can you think of one?

Tracy: We were skidding on ice once and my dad couldn't steer the car and it skidded all over the road. Then my dad got it to stop just before we ran into a tree and my mom said that our guardian angel was with us. Maybe even a couple of angels. Can you think of some time when God saved you from something that was very scary or dangerous?

Let your puppets take it from here.

A Bible Verse to Learn

With God all things are possible. Matthew 19:26

Talk to God

God cares just as much about you today as He did about those people way back in Bible times. Thank Him for this, and thank Him for every time you can think of when He saved you from harm. Ask God to help you remember to pray to Him when you are in trouble.

Can You Find This Story in the Bible?

Find Exodus 12:29-51; 14:1-31; 15:1-21.

The Grumble-Mumble People

Moses and the Hebrew people were safe on the other side of the Red Sea. God had promised to lead them to a wonderful land. But first they had to go through a wilderness. No trees. No gardens. No roads. No houses. No stores. No water. Just wilderness.

They followed the pillar of cloud on—and on—and ON. And after awhile they began to get thirsty. And they began to grumble. "Water!" they cried. Grumble-mumble-grumble. "We should have stayed in Egypt." Grumble-mumble. And then—

"Water!" someone shouted, up ahead. And they all rushed up ahead, to see. Sure enough, there was water—beautiful, wet water, shining in the sun! They shouted for joy— they ran toward it— they cupped their hands and drank some—and aughhhhhhhhhh! It was BITTER! It was so bitter they couldn't possibly drink it.

And then they did a shameful thing. They forgot how good God had been to them and they began to grumble.

"Are you trying to kill us?" they cried as they screwed up their faces. "We should have stayed in Egypt," they wailed as they puckered up their lips.

But Moses didn't grumble. He knew that GOD could help them. So instead of grumbling, he asked God what to do. And God told him. And this is what Moses did.

He went to look for a tree. Not just ANY old tree. It was a SPECIAL tree God had told him about. And he—hup—got that tree and brought it back to the water. And the people watched. And he—hup! Threw it into the water. And the people watched. And they waited. And then Moses said, "Drink!"

They went—up—to—the—water—and—tasted it, just a LITTLE. Sip. Then they tasted it again. More, this time. GULP.

It was sweet. It was pure. It was DELICIOUS!

They drank and DRANK. And for awhile, they were happy again. They followed the cloud on and ON. And after awhile, their food was all used up. They began to be hungry. And again they began to grumble. "Food!" they cried. Grumble-mumble-grumble. "Do you want to kill us? We should have stayed in Egypt!"

But Moses didn't grumble. Again he asked God what to do. And when God had told him, he called all the people together.

"Why do you grumble?" cried Moses. "God is still taking care of you. At night you shall have meat to eat—and in the morning, God will rain down bread from heaven for you!"

Meat! Bread from heaven! They stopped grumbling, and waited. And when evening came—

Suddenly, thousands and thousands of birds, called quail, came flying across the sky. So many of them that they looked like a huge black cloud. And flying so low that the people could reach right up with their hands and catch them! They ate and ATE.

And next morning when they got up—there all over the ground—were little white round things that looked like seeds. "Manna?" they wanted to know. (Manna means "What is it?")

"It's the bread from heaven that God promised you," said Moses.

"Manna?" they said, as they tasted it. It was sweet, like little cakes made with honey. "Manna!" they cried, as they gathered it. It was GOOD.

"You must gather only as much as you need each day," said Moses. "And you must gather it early in the morning."

But some of the people disobeyed. "There might not BE any here tomorrow morning," they said. Grumble-mumble. And they gathered a lot extra. But the next day, all that they had left over— was SPOILED.

And some of the people were lazy. "Early in the morning is too EARLY," they said. Mumble-grumble. And they waited till later in the day. But the sun came out and melted the manna—and later in the day—it was GONE.

On the day before the Sabbath, Moses told the people they must gather TWICE as much, and God wouldn't let it spoil. For on the Sabbath, God wanted them to rest. Sure enough—the manna didn't spoil—and sure enough—on the Sabbath, there wasn't any manna on the ground.

And so—even though they were the grumbliest-mumbliest people you could imagine—God took care of them and fed them every day. But they had to follow His instructions and obey Him— or they didn't have any food to thank Him FOR!

Tracy and Mike Talk It Over

Mike: After all that God did for His people, all they did was grumble-mumble. It's hard to say that fast. Grumblemumblegrumblemumble. Can you say murmur? Murmurmurmur—

Tracy: I can't say it fast without giggling.

Mike: When do you grumble the most?

Tracy: When my dad and mom say, "Turn off the TV now." I can watch only two hours. But I can choose which programs.

Mike: I grumble when Mom says, "Clean up your room."

Tracy: I don't like it when my teacher says, "You'll have to wait your turn."

Mike: Yeah—I hate that too. I hate ALL that stuff. I OBEY on the OUTSIDE—but on the INSIDE I can hear my grumble-mumbles clear down to my toes.

Tracy: But once I decide to obey CHEERFULLY, it doesn't seem so hard. I feel good inside when I obey cheerfully.

Mike: Besides it gives your parents a shock.

Let the puppets take it from here.

Help them think of their own grumble-mumble areas, and how they can be more cheerful when they FEEL grumbly-mumbly.

A Bible Verse to Learn

Do everything without complaining or arguing. Philippians 2:14

Talk to God

See how many things you can think of to thank God for. And when you've finished with that, ask Him to forgive you for all the times you have grumbled. Can you promise Him that you'll try to cut down on the grumbling?

Can You Find This Story in the Bible?

Find Exodus 15:22-27; 16:1-35.

The Laws that Lasted Forever

Now a lot of important things happened to Moses and his people as they wandered through the wilderness, but one of the most IMPORTANT things was what happened in this story.

A wonderful part of the journey through the wilderness was the pillar of cloud. No matter what happened to Moses and the Hebrew people, it was always there. When it moved, they followed it. And when it stopped—they stopped and put up their tents. It was low enough for them to see. But not low enough for them to reach. They couldn't touch it, or get up inside it to see what it was like. It was a great mystery. It looked as if nobody was EVER going to really get close to that cloud. But one day—somebody did! And that somebody was Moses!

It happened this way.

One day the people saw a great mountain in the distance. The pillar of cloud went toward the mountain. Closer, closer. And the people followed. And then the cloud got right on TOP of the mountain—and stopped. The people all stopped too, and put up their tents, and camped all around the foot of the mountain. It was Mount Sinai.

Many people think this is Mount Sinai. Can you picture the people of Israel setting up their tents near this mountain? Can you picture Moses climbing up, up, up this mountain? And can you picture Moses coming down again with the laws from God? (Photo © Frances Blankenbaker)

111

One day, after they were all settled, Moses told the people he was going up into the mountain—alone. He said good-bye, and they watched him go—

climbing up, up, UP

and getting smaller and smaller—

until he was just a speck.

While Moses was on the mountain, God called to him. "Moses!" God said, "I have a message for you to give to the people."

Moses listened carefully to God's message, and then he went down to give the message to the people.

When the leaders of the people were gathered together, Moses said, "You know how good God has been to us. He has helped us every time we've been in trouble. NOW—"

"Now—WHAT?" the people wondered.

"NOW—" said Moses, "God wants US to do something for HIM. He wants us to belong to Him in a VERY SPECIAL way. And He wants to give us a SET OF LAWS—so we will know how He wants us to live. And you may have your CHOICE. Do you want these laws or not?"

Did they want the laws? Oh YES! "Tell God we'll do anything He says!" they cried.

So Moses went back up the mountain to tell God. And when he came back down he had something even MORE IMPORTANT to say. "You must get all cleaned up," he said, "and wash your clothes. For in three days God is coming right to the mountain. He'll be RIGHT HERE."

Oh MY!

Everybody got busy at once. They cleaned the camp. They washed their clothes. They washed themselves. And then they waited. And sure enough—

The lightning FLASHED!   The thunder CRASHED!

A mysterious trumpet BLEW!   And the mountain SHOOK!

And SMOKED!   And TREMBLED!

The people trembled, too. They backed up and BACKED UP—until they were a safe distance away. And there they waited—frightened.

But Moses went right up into the mountain and INTO THE

SMOKE, to get the set of laws from God. And when he came back—

Sure enough, he told them all the laws God wanted them to obey. "We will obey!" the people shouted. "All that God says we will obey!"

And do you know, those laws have lasted right up until today—for they are the TEN COMMANDMENTS we have in the Bible! They are lasting forever—or at least until Jesus comes back again!

Tracy and Mike Talk It Over

Tracy: Why do you think the people all had to wash themselves and put on clean clothes and clean up their messes?

Mike: I suppose God had to remind the people that He is HOLY. He had to do that every once in awhile.

Tracy: Well, my mom says that we should remember TODAY how holy God is.

Mike: When did she tell you that?

Tracy: When she caught me running through the church sanctuary with a Popsicle in my hand.

Mike: I remember SOME of the Ten Commandments. Honor your father and mother—put God ahead of everything—don't lie—don't steal. Can you think of any more?

Let your puppets take it from here.

(Parent/teacher: Guide children to discuss one or two commands they can work on obeying this week.)

A Bible Verse to Learn

I will obey your word. Psalm 119:17

Talk to God

Thank God for giving us His commands. Ask Him to help you obey them cheerfully.

Can You Find This Story in the Bible?

Find Exodus 19:1-25; 20:1-21; 24:1-3.

Two
Against
Ten

The Hebrew people thought their journey would NEVER end!
They marched and stopped and marched again and waited and
WAITED. And then, suddenly—there it was! The Promised Land.
Just a few miles away!

The pillar of cloud stopped. The people stopped. They
unpacked their things—and waited for God to tell them what to do.
And He did.

"God has told me to send spies into the land," Moses told the
people.

Spies?

"Yes," said Moses, "I'm going to send twelve spies to look
over the land and come back and tell us what they saw."

Everyone talked at once. Spies—into the new land! It wouldn't
be long now!

They talked about it while Moses chose twelve strong men to
go. They talked about it while Moses gave the men their
instructions. They talked about it while the twelve men said good-
bye to their families and started off. And they were still talking
about it when the men left, and disappeared—just specks in the
distance. The Promised Land!

The people could hardly wait.

They looked and listened and talked about it. Ten days went by. What would the men find? Twenty days went by. How would the men be treated? Thirty days went by. What would the men have to tell when they got back? Thirty-five days went by. What if they DIDN'T come back? Ohhhhhhhh. Forty days went by. And then—

"They're coming, they're coming!" The shout went up all over the camp. And sure enough—first just specks in the distance—and then—the men—all twelve of them. They were safe! The people gathered around.

"There was fruit in the land," the spies said, and they swung a big pole off their shoulders with a bunch of grapes tied to it—nearly as big as a wheelbarrow! "There are figs and pomegranates too," they said, and they took out of their packs fruit such as the people had never seen before. "And there's grass—and water—and grain—everything!" they said—"BUT—!"

Everybody was quiet. Ten of the spies scowled. "We can't go," they said.

Can't go? The people's hearts almost stopped.

"We can't go over," the men went on. "The people are strong and BIG—almost like GIANTS. And their cities have high walls that nearly reach to the sky. They'll kill us all. We can't go over!"

"Wait!"

It was the two other spies. Their names were Joshua and Caleb. "Wait!" they said, and they held up their hands. The people listened.

"We CAN go!" said Caleb. "God is with us. We needn't be afraid. Let's go!"

"No!" shouted the other spies.

"God will help us!" said Joshua and Caleb.

And the ten spies shouted and the people shouted, until you couldn't hear Joshua or Caleb at all.

"We can't go!" shouted the ten spies. And the people answered, "That's right! We can't go!"

And they didn't.

Those foolish people stayed in the wilderness. They stayed for years and YEARS. There was the Promised Land they'd been waiting for—but they didn't go over because they were afraid. And there was God, waiting to help them—but they didn't let Him—because they didn't believe!

116

Tracy and Mike Talk It Over

Tracy: How do you think YOU'D feel if you heard the spies say there were people like giants in the new land? Have you ever been afraid?

Mike: NAW—I'm NEVER afraid.

Tracy: Oh come on now, Mike. You must get scared—sometimes.

Mike: Welllll—sometimes. A little bit.

Tracy: But it's OKAY to be afraid. Even grown-ups are afraid sometimes. You're supposed to ask God to help you. My dad says EVERYBODY is afraid once in awhile.

Mike: Well I'll tell you about a time when I was afraid, if you'll tell me a time when YOU were.

Let your puppets take it from here.

(Parent/teacher: Suggest hypothetical frightening situations if children can't think of real ones. And whatever they "act out," remind them to ask God for help.)

Some Bible Verses to Learn

God says, *Do not fear, for I am with you.* Isaiah 41:10
   "I myself will help you," declares the LORD. Isaiah 41:14
   When I am afraid, I will trust in you. Psalm 56:3

Talk to God

Thank God that He knows you get frightened sometimes. EVERYBODY does. Thank Him that it is NOT A SIN to be afraid. And thank Him for His promise to help you.

Can You Find This Story in the Bible?

Find Numbers 13:16-31.

How Does God Fight His Battles? Any Way He Wants To!

The people of God had spent many, many years in the wilderness. It was time now to go into the land that God had promised them. But on their way, they had to capture the wicked, WICKED city of Jericho. The people of God were called Israelites. Their leader Moses was dead and their NEW leader was a man named Joshua. (Do you remember him from the last story?) And the battle they fought at Jericho was the strangest battle the world has ever known.

At Joshua's command, Israel's army marched toward Jericho. First there were soldiers with swords and shields and bows and arrows and slings and spears. But then—what was this? Holy men all dressed in white—seven of them, and they carried trumpets made from rams' horns.

TRUMPETS?!?

Yes, trumpets. And behind them, more men dressed in white, and behind them more soldiers.

What kind of army was THIS! It was WEIRD. What were they up to?

Well, they marched up to the gates of Jericho and then turned and started marching around the city wall. And as they marched,

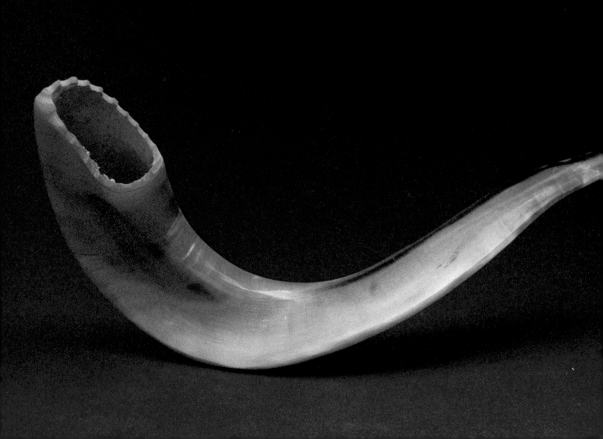

the men with the rams' horn trumpets blew them.

The bone-chilling blast of the trumpets split the air and bounced against the walls and echoed all over the plains!

The army marched all the way around the city and then—when the first soldiers got back to where they'd started—they marched away—back across the plains!

What were they up to? And what kind of battle was this? And how does the God of Israel fight His battles anyhow?

Nobody knew but Joshua.

Nobody in Jericho could sleep that night. They all watched and waited.

The next morning at dawn, Joshua's army went out again, just the way it had the day before, the same trumpet blasts and the same marching away in silence. Well, this was ridiculous, the people inside Jericho thought. How long was this going to go on?

Well it went on the next day.

And the next.

And the next. FOR SIX MORNINGS!

And then it was the seventh day. It began just like the other six days.

But wait! When the army had gone around the city once, they didn't march away. They just kept on going around the city wall. They marched around a second time—then a third time— a fourth time—a fifth time—a sixth time—then they started around for the SEVENTH TIME—

The trumpets—the trumpets—the TRUMPETS! Loud enough to pop your eardrums!

Then Joshua shouted at the people, "Shout" he cried, "SHOUT, for the Lord has given us this city!" Then everybody in the whole army shouted probably using the same words, "THE LORD HAS GIVEN US THIS CITY! JERICHO IS OURS IN THE NAME OF THE LORD!!!"

The first photo shows how Jericho looks today—it is an oasis (grassy place) in a wilderness area. The mound in the foreground is part of the ruins of biblical Jericho. (Photo © Gil Beers) When Joshua's army marched around Jericho, the holy men in white (the priests) carried trumpets made from rams' horns—like the one in the second photo. (Photo © Tim Howard)

And then another noise rumbled up from the earth,
   louder than the shouting.
The walls! The WALLS!
   Big jagged cracks zigzagged their way up the outer walls.
      The walls groaned, they snapped, they tore.
         Then they lurched crazily outward—
            ripping and crashing and tearing
               and sprawling down the hillside!

And the orders went forth just as God had given them to Joshua, and the Israelites poured into the city from every side.

The battle was won! The wicked city of Jericho was conquered!

It surely was a strange way to fight a battle. But if you'd been there and asked Joshua how does God fight His battles, Joshua would probably have answered, "ANY WAY HE PLEASES! "

Tracy and Mike Talk It Over

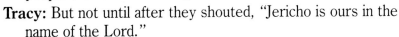

Tracy: Whew! That's the strangest battle I've ever heard about.

Mike: And they won it! Joshua and his people won the battle of Jericho.

Tracy: But not until after they shouted, "Jericho is ours in the name of the Lord."

Mike: My dad says that we should still pray to God like that today. We should pray in Jesus' name. Can you think of things you can ask Him to do today in Jesus' name?

Tracy: Well, I don't ask Him to knock walls down, but some of the problems I have seem just as big and just as hard. They might as well be walls. Can you think of something?

Let your puppets take it from here.

(Parent/teacher: Help children think about times they need God's help in times of difficulty.)

A Bible Verse to Learn

In everything, by prayer . . . present your requests to God.
Philippians 4:6

Talk to God

Maybe you have a problem that seems too hard for you to handle by yourself. Why don't you ask Jesus about it right now? Maybe He has a solution you haven't thought of. And don't forget to thank Him.

Can You Find This Story in the Bible?

Find Joshua 6:1-20.

The Day the Sun Stood Still

ATTACK!!!

What? Another battle?

Yes. Joshua and his army were still marching through Canaan, wiping out the wicked people who lived there, so that the Israelites could settle down in the Promised Land that God had given them.

If you think that battle back in Jericho was a strange one—wait 'til you hear about this one.

But what a mad scramble it was! On and on the soldiers fought all morning long. And hot! In that part of the country at that time of the year, it was 120° in the shade.

One problem.

No shade!

The scorching sun beat down on them without mercy.

It was the enemy armies who gave up first. They broke ranks and started scrambling madly away. And Joshua stood still and looked after them. The sweat was streaming down his face. His tongue was thick with thirst. His knees were wobbly. But with what strength he had left, he cried out to his soldiers, "After them!"

Not a man stirred. He cried out again, "After themmmmmmm!"

But his soldiers stared back at him and then their eyes rolled back in their heads. And their tongues hung out. And then they dropped in their tracks with heat and exhaustion. They tried to get up, but they moved in slow motion—and sank back down again.

It looked hopeless. And Joshua said, "God—help us." And it didn't come out like a big brave shout either, it came out like more of a gurgle. Joshua had hardly one drop of strength left in him.

And then—

What was this? A black cloud came over the sun! And though it never rained in that country through the summer months, it not only rained—

It HAILED!

God never does anything by halves, He had turned on a mighty air conditioner! And Joshua's soldiers, one by one and two by two, sat up where they had dropped. They scraped up chunks of hail. They popped them in their mouths. They put them down their necks. They rubbed their faces with them. WOOOEEE! They were ready to go again.

They chased the enemy down across the plains and through the narrow rocky mountain passes, tailgating them all the way.

And the Bible tells us that the hailstones killed more of the enemy than the swords of Joshua's army did. And the chase went on and on—long after the hailstorm had stopped.

And the day was wearing on and on, too—the late afternoon shadows were beginning to fall across the rocks, getting longer and longer. The job wasn't over yet and it was beginning to look as if it wasn't going to get done before nightfall.

It was then that Joshua asked God to do something that was hard to believe—it was a headspinner!

"Oh, God, help me!" he cried, and he looked up at the sun, and over across the valley where a pale moon rode in the sky.

"Let the sun stand still" he cried. "And you, too, moon, stand still in your place."

WHAAAAT!?

Joshua was asking God to stop time!

And God did!

Yes! It tells us in the Bible that the sun stopped in its tracks in the heavens—and stayed where it was FOR ABOUT 24 HOURS!

And the sun and the moon
did not move until Joshua
and his armies finished
the job they had begun!

Never had there been a day like it before and never has there been one like it since when God stopped the sun and the moon—
Because one man asked Him to!

Tracy and Mike Talk It Over

Mike: I don't see how God could have stopped the sun. Do you really think He could?

Tracy: Sure He could. He made it, didn't He? As He says in the Bible, "Is anything too hard for me?" (Jeremiah 32:27).

Mike: I guess nothing is. But why doesn't God do big stuff like that for us today?

Tracy: Maybe because it wouldn't be good for us. He does things for us that we really need. Supposing you asked Him to do something for you that would be dangerous, and you didn't know it, but He knew it because He can see what's ahead. Did you ever ask Him to do something and He didn't do it?—And then later on you were GLAD He didn't do it?

Mike: Hmmmm. I see what you mean. I'll try to think of something.

Let your puppets take it from here.

A Bible Verse to Learn

Lord, you have made the heavens and the earth by your great power and outstretched arm. Nothing is too hard for you. Jeremiah 32:17

Talk to God

Thank God that He knows what's ahead. If He doesn't do what you ask Him to do, there is always a very good reason.

Can You Find This Story in the Bible?

Find Joshua 10:7-15.

The Choice that Brought Many Surprises

Ruth? RUTH? Who was SHE?

Well she was nobody when her story begins. She lived in the country of Moab.

Now the people in Moab worshiped the God Chemosh—an IDOL. They gave gifts to this big stone idol. And they offered him sacrifices. They even burnt their children and offered them to their great idol Chemosh.

Of course they knew all about the big country of Judea, fifty miles away from them, and they knew all about the people who lived there. They knew that the people in Judea were called Hebrews and that they worshiped a living God.

Of course, Ruth did not believe in this living God, and neither did her friend Orpah. Ruth and Orpah had been brought up to worship the idol Chemosh. And that was that. Or that would have been that except for one thing.

Women today still work in the grain fields of Bethlehem, just as Ruth did in Bible times. Ruth was a gleaner—someone who was allowed to gather up what was left on the ground after the stalks had been cut and tied into bundles. (Photo © Stacey Martin)

A Hebrew family came over from Bethlehem in the country of Judea and moved into Moab. The father's name was Elimelech. The mother's name was Naomi and they had two sons, and their names were Mahlon and Chilion. And THAT would have been that also except for one thing.

Ruth and Orpah wound up falling in love with the two sons. Now it was the custom in those days that when a girl got married, she went to live in the home of her husband. So Ruth and Orpah moved in with Mahlon and Chilion and Elimelech and Naomi.

Naomi! What a mother-in-law SHE was! Was she ever bossy! "Worship the idol Chemosh!," she raged. "Not in this house they don't. In this house we will worship the living God!" And that's where it all would have ended, except for one thing. Well—THREE things.

Elimelech fell sick—and died.

And Mahlon and Chilion fell sick—and died.

And there was no one left in that little family except Ruth and Orpah—and Naomi. They were all widows—women whose husbands had died.

Well, Naomi decided that she wanted to go back to Bethlehem and take her two new daughters with her. So they packed up a couple of donkeys and started the long trek back to Bethlehem.

But they had not gone very far, when Naomi changed her mind. "Go back, my daughters," she said. "Go back to your own country. I'll never be able to find new husbands for you in Bethlehem."

Well that made sense to Orpah, but it didn't make sense to Ruth. For she had learned to love this bossy mother-in-law, and she had come to believe in this LIVING GOD.

"Please don't ask me to go back," she pleaded. "Let me go on with you. Where you go, I will go. Your people will be my people, and your God will be my God."

So Orpah went back to Moab and Ruth went on with Naomi.

Ruth did not know it then, but her story was just beginning.

After Ruth and Naomi settled down in a little house in Bethlehem, Ruth had to get busy and find food for them to eat. The place to go was one of the barley fields.

Now in the barley fields, the reapers went ahead and cut the barley down. Then came the BINDERS. They stood the barley stalks on end and tied them into bundles. And then came the

130

GLEANERS. They were the ones who were allowed to gather up the stalks that were spilled and left on the ground. They were the POOR people. And the WIDOWS. Like Ruth.

So Ruth gathered the end of her outer robe into a pouch and picked up barley stalks and stuffed them in. She was stuffing away when suddenly there was a hush all over the barley field.

Ruth looked up with shock and fear. There, standing in the field was the owner of the field—Boaz. Ruth was from Moab—would he chase her off his field?

And then Ruth heard Boaz call out to his workers, "The Lord be with you." And they called back, "The Lord bless you." And THEN—

Boaz came over to Ruth.

She bowed low before him. She still thought he might ask her to leave, but instead he said, "I have heard how good you have been to Naomi, and I've instructed my binders to leave extra stalks of barley for you to glean."

Wooooeeeeey! Ruth went home that night with her pouch stuffed to over flowing and told Naomi all about it.

"Boaz!" Naomi cried. "Why he is one of Elimelech's relatives.

This means you have a right to claim him as a HUSBAND."

"Motherrrr!" Ruth said, "I could NEVER do that!"

"Ruth," Naomi said sternly, "it's LEGAL. It's an old Hebrew custom. I'll show you just what you must do.

"But we must wait until harvesttime. You will do it during the harvest feast."

And what Naomi told Ruth to do was astonishing. It sent Ruth's head aspinning!

Tracy and Mike Talk It Over

Mike: Ruth had a hard choice to make. She didn't know what she was getting into.

Tracy: No, but she knew what she was getting out of. She was getting out of Moab, where they worshiped idols.

Mike: Was she choosing Naomi or was she choosing God?

Tracy: I think she was choosing God. Well, maybe both, but mostly God.

Mike: Supposing you had to choose between two things. Maybe two places to go. One way meant getting away from God, and one way meant getting closer to God. Can you think of any time like that?

Let your puppets take it from here.

Help them think of times when they want to do things that would keep them from going to church or studying the Bible.

A Bible Verse to Learn

We will serve the Lord our God and obey him. Joshua 24:24

Talk to God

Thank God that He is willing to help you make your choices. Sometimes it's hard for you to go the way God chooses for you, because the other way looks like more fun. Ask Him to help you make the right choices.

Can You Find This Story in the Bible?

Find Ruth 1:1-22; 2:1-23.

A Daring Plan—Would It Work?

The Harvest Feast! What an exciting time THAT was! The bundles of barley were carried over to the threshing floor* in carts. Then came teams of oxen, dragging huge sleds. One of the workers stood on the front of the sled, driving the oxen, and some of the children sat behind. They thought they were getting a jolly ride, but actually they were needed to weigh the sled down so it would be heavier in rolling over the grain. The sleds went over the stalks of grain with a great scraping noise, rubbing the kernels off and grinding the stalks to bits. Then the barley was sifted and put in HUGE PILES. And while all this was going on, the people were shouting and laughing and the children were playing tag around the edges of the field and it didn't seem like work at all!

They all worked until it began to get dark, and then—

The feast!

Now the fun REALLY began. The people gathered in groups, sitting on the ground around the edge of the field and all the food they had brought was passed around. Such laughing and merry-making you cannot imagine!

And then came the singing!

Such singing it was!

---

*The threshing floor was a field that had been rolled and tromped down until it was as hard as could be.

Some of the songs were happy songs and the people clapped their hands and swayed back and forth. Some of the songs were sad songs. But every song told a story. They told about Joseph and Moses and all the people God had used down through the years. And every song, glad or sad, told about God's great love for His people.

Then bit by bit the singing died down. Many of the people left to go home. And those who stayed behind, bedded down alongside the huge piles of barley, to guard it from thieves. And they covered themselves with their outer cloaks. And finally the singing stopped. And the laughing. And the talking. Until there was no sound but the night bugs.

Ruth sat perfectly still, waiting until everybody was asleep. Now was the time to do what Naomi had told her to do. She got to her feet and started toward the place where she saw Boaz sleeping. "O Lord," she thought, "don't let me stumble over anybody." She crept along in the dark until she was at last sitting beside Boaz.

Now.

She picked up a corner of his cloak—*Careful now, careful.* And then she lay down at his feet—woops—CAREFUL! *And she pulled his cloak up over her shoulder.*

And then Boaz awoke.

Ruth's heart began to POUND.

"Who is it?" he whispered.

"It's Ruth," she whispered back.

Boaz got up on one elbow and so did Ruth. The cloak slid from her shoulders. She swallowed hard once. Twice. And then she

found her voice. "Spread your cloak back over me, Boaz," she said, "for you are my nearest relative."

There. It was out.

And joy of joys—Boaz wasn't angry. He was HAPPY. For it turned out that he had been in love with Ruth all along—but she was so young and so beautiful he never DREAMED she would want to marry him.

It was a harvest feast neither Boaz nor Ruth would ever forget!* And there were more surprises ahead!

Tracy and Mike Talk It Over

Tracy: I can't wait to hear about the wedding.
Mike: Aw, that's a lot of mushy stuff.
Tracy: No! My mom told me it's more than that! Weddings were exciting in those days. It'll be at least as much fun as the harvest feast. EVERYBODY takes part!
Mike: I sure like the harvest feast. Do we ever have times like that—when people get together to sing and have fun and eat?
Tracy: Maybe our church picnic. We sit around and sing when it's over.

Let your puppets take it from here.

Have your puppets think of some times when working together can be made fun—like a church "clean up" time or raking autumn leaves.

A Bible Verse to Learn

Give thanks to the Lord, for he is good. Psalm 136:1

Talk to God

Thank God for the good times He provides—when you can have fun working together with other people.

Can You Find This Story in the Bible?

Find Ruth 3:1-11.

---

*You can read more about this in "Great Heroes of the Bible" Series by Ethel Barrett.

An Impossible
Dream
Comes True!

A wedding!
The news spread all over town!

Boaz—one of the richest men in Bethlehem. And Ruth—the beautiful Moabite girl!

Naomi and her friends scrubbed Ruth to a stand-still and washed and brushed her hair until it shone like satin. Then they dressed her in the beautiful clothes and jewels Boaz had sent.

And at last the evening came.

Shouts, out in the street! And music! Coming up the street was Boaz with singers and musicians and friends.

When he got to the gate, Naomi and Ruth were waiting for him. He took Ruth's hands. And together Ruth and Boaz turned down the crooked streets and the whole wedding procession followed them, with their oil lamps, like a great streak of light, all the way back to Boaz's house. And a feast! And the laughing and the shouting and the singing echoed over the hills of Bethlehem and out to the dark fields beyond, where Ruth's new life had really begun. And Ruth thought, "I shall never be happier in all my life!"

But she was. For a year later, her most impossible dream came true. It was Naomi's impossible dream, too. Can you guess what it was?

Of course, a baby!

When Boaz saw his newborn child, he swooped him up in his arms and held him high over his head and shouted, "I HAVE A SON!"

Then he turned to Naomi and laid the child in her arms. "You have a grandson at last, Naomi," he said. And Naomi opened her robe and snuggled the baby inside. And Ruth and Naomi looked at each other with love.

What rejoicing there was after that! The friends and neighbors came and the singing began all over again.

"Bless the Lord!"

"Bless Ruth, too!"

"May this child be famous in all of Israel!"

And they named the child Obed.

They did not know that Obed would grow up and have a son—
And name him Jesse.

And that Jesse would grow up and have a son—
And name him David.
And that David would grow up to be DAVID THE KING!
And that from David's family would come—
The Lord Jesus Christ Himself!
So Ruth, a little Moabite girl, turned out to be one of the most important women in the whole Bible!

Tracy and Mike Talk It Over

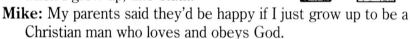

Tracy: I wonder if I'll be somebody special when I grow up, like Ruth.

Mike: My parents said they'd be happy if I just grow up to be a Christian man who loves and obeys God.

Tracy: Do you suppose Billy Graham's Sunday School teacher knew that he was going to grow up to be a great preacher?

Mike: I don't suppose so. When you're going to grow up to be that great, I guess you have to start pretty young.

Tracy: I guess the important thing is to be willing to do what God wants you to do.

Mike: How can you know what God wants you to do?

Have your puppets take if from here.

A Bible Verse to Learn

Show me your ways, O Lord, teach me your paths. Psalm 25:4

Talk to God

Thank God for giving you the Bible that tells what He wants you to do—and for giving you parents, grandparents, teachers and others who help you learn what God wants you to do. Ask God to help you obey Him now and as you continue to grow. Thank God that He has a plan for your life.

Can You Find This Story in the Bible?

Find Ruth 4:13-22.

The Giant Killer

It started out to be a pretty exciting adventure for David. His father had sent him to the battle field where his older brothers were fighting in King Saul's army against the wicked Philistines.

When David got there, he found the two armies camped on two hills with a valley between them. He nuggled his way through the soldiers of King Saul's army, looking for his brothers.

But what was going on?

What he heard, stopped him in his tracks.

This was not going to be a big battle after all. It was going to be a CONTEST. They were going to choose two soldiers—one from each army—to fight it out with each other! And the soldier who won the contest by killing the OTHER soldier, would win the battle for his whole army!

David stood stock still and listened. And watched.

Everyone was silent, waiting. And gawking at the Philistine army on the other side of the hill.

A giant of a man was there.

A giant! Why, he was over nine feet tall! His armor must have weighed over 200 pounds! And his spear was as big as a weaver's beam with an iron spearhead that must have weighed 25 pounds if it weighed an ounce!

David's jaw dropped, and as he stood there, his eyes nearly bulged out of his head. He could not believe what he was seeing. THIS was the soldier the Philistines had sent? Who would dare to fight him?

David watched as the giant raised his huge arm in the air and everybody got very, very quiet. "Do you need a whole army to settle this?" the giant bellowed. "Choose a soldier for yourselves and send him out here. We'll settle this right now."

No one moved.

"If your soldier is able to kill me—you win! But if I kill him—we win!"

David turned to the soldiers around him, "Who is this giant?" he asked.

"His name is Goliath. He comes here every morning and insults our armies. No one is brave enough to fight him."

No one dares to fight him? David thought. *No one dares to fight him?!?*

And he shouted, "Who does this Philistine think he is, that he is allowed to talk this way to the armies of the living God?"

The soldiers gathered around him. Who was this kid anyhow who was talking like a king? Was he serious? Was he saying that HE would fight the giant?

Yes, that's exactly what David was saying. And when King Saul heard about it and called for David, David said to him, "Don't trouble yourself, O king, about the giant Goliath. I'll go out and fight him." Both sides watched as David left King Saul's tent and then stopped alongside a small brook and took five stones. They saw him open his shepherd's bag and put the stones inside. Everyone watched as David started toward the giant, armed with only his staff and his sling! Everyone was thinking—why that giant is so BIG—how can David ever hit him?

But David was thinking—why that giant's so big, how can I ever MISS him?

And the giant Goliath was thinking—is this the soldier who

David fought Goliath in the Valley of Elah (first photo). He used a shepherd's sling (second photo) to hurl the stone at Goliath. Can you picture David and Goliath facing each other in this valley hundreds of years ago? (Photos © Joyce Thimsen, Tim Howard)

thinks he can fight me? This KID? "Am I a dog" he bellowed, "that you come at me with a stick?"

David kept on marching toward Goliath.

"Come here!" the giant howled. "And I'll feed you to the birds!"

"You come at me with a sword and a spear," David shouted back. "But I come to you IN THE NAME OF THE LORD! Today the Lord will conquer you!"

The giant Goliath sputtered with rage. "The battle is the Lord's," David was shouting. "He will deliver you into our hands." David loaded his sling, took aim, slung his sling in a circle and he let it go—

P-F-F-F-F-F-F-T—

The stone streaked through the air, sure and true—and hit Goliath square between the eyes with a—

THUNK!!!!

It sank into Goliath's forehead and the blood spurted out and ran down his face. The giant looked astonished for a minute and then he tottered forward and fell. And hit the ground with a THWACK!

There was a shocked, shocked silence. The Philistine army could not believe that the giant Goliath had fallen. The Israelite army couldn't believe that David had done it.

David—the shepherd boy—killed the giant Goliath.

And won the battle for the king of Israel!

Tracy and Mike Talk It Over

Mike: Wow! David killed that big ole' giant with just a little ole' SLINGSHOT.

Tracy: Would you be afraid to face the giant if all you had was a slingshot?

Mike: I'd be afraid to face a giant if I had TEN slingshots. Anyhow, I think God gave David a special dose of super courage. So he wasn't afraid to do it.

Tracy: Why would God do that?

Mike: Well, because He had a special job for David to do and He gave him the courage to do it. My dad told me once that our problems are like giants. And that we can face them just the same as David faced the giant Goliath.

Tracy: Did you ever have a problem that seemed as big as a giant? Let the puppets take it from here.

Help them think of problems that seem as BIG as giants—like needing courage to do right when everyone else is doing wrong.

A Bible Verse to Learn

Be strong and courageous . . . . For the Lord your God will be with you wherever you go. Joshua 1:9

Talk to God

Thank God that He is willing to help you with your problems, even though they do seem like giants. And if you have a problem right now, tell God about it. He likes to have you talk things over with Him. He cares about all your problems—big or little!

Can You Find This Story in the Bible?

Find 1 Samuel 17:1-51.

A Sad Good-bye

David had killed the giant! He was no longer known as David the shepherd boy, he was now known as the FEARLESS SOLDIER! The people sang his praises, they had parades for him. His best friend in all the world was—

King Saul's own son—PRINCE JONATHAN.

Well, it looked as if everybody was going to live happily ever after, didn't it? And that's the way David and Jonathan wanted it to be. But that's not the way it was.

For Jonathan's father, King Saul—became JEALOUS.

The more people praised David, the more jealous the king became. At first, it was sad. Then it was miserable. Then it was DANGEROUS.

It was SO dangerous, in fact, that David was afraid jealous King Saul would KILL him.

When David talked to Prince Jonathan about this, Jonathan said, "I'll see what I can find out. But you had better hide until I can get a message to you."

Then David and Jonathan made a secret PLAN.

"The day after tomorrow," said Jonathan, "come and hide out here in the field. When I have found out if your life is in danger, I'll come out for some target practice with my bow and arrows and I'll bring a boy with me."

David nodded his head.

"I'll shoot three arrows," Jonathan said, "as if I'm shooting at a target. Got it?"

"Got it."

"Now," Jonathan went on, "if I shoot the arrows in FRONT of that stone, I'll shout to the boy, 'They're on this side.' That will mean every thing is all right, BUT—

"If I shoot them PAST the stone, I'll tell the boy to go

farther—'go FARTHER—they're still up ahead of you.' I'll SHOUT IT so you'll be sure to hear."

David shook his head sadly, "I know," he said, "that will mean I have to run away."

"It means you'll have to run for your life," Jonathan said. "My father can get very angry."

And was Jonathan ever right!

A few days later King Saul exploded in such a rage that the whole palace seemed to tremble. "Go find that good-for-nothing David and bring him here," he shouted. "I'll have his hide!"

It was so bad—it was so BAD—that Jonathan knew the time had come to carry out his secret PLAN with David.

He took a servant boy with him and went off to practice shooting arrows. And he headed straight for the field where David was hiding. When he got near the stone marker, he stopped and placed an arrow in his bow. "All right, start running," he told the servant boy. He sent the arrow zinging through the air and the servant ran after it. Then Jonathan put another arrow in his bow. He pulled the string WAAAAAY back and shot the arrow—ZING! Right over the boy's head and PAST THE STONE MARKER.

That was the signal. Then, as the boy got up to the FIRST ARROW that had been shot, Jonathan shouted with all his might, "No—NO! Go on, go ON! I shot that one way up ahead of you. Go ON!"

The servant boy ran PAST the stone and picked up the arrow. "All right," Jonathan told the boy, "you can go back to the palace now. I'm finished with my practice." And the boy went back to the palace.

So, it looked as if Jonathan had just been out for target practice. No one could suspect that he was there to warn his best friend.

And in a minute—out scrambled David. The two best friends put their hands on each other's shoulders and the tears ran down their cheeks. And right then and there, they gave their friendship and themselves—to God. "Remember, David," Jonathan said, "we've given ourselves to God forever, and He will take care of us."

"Yes, He will," David said. "And we'll always be best friends, Jonathan, forever."

And do you know what?

They WERE best friends for all the rest of their lives.

Tracy and Mike Talk It Over

Tracy: Boy, they were really friends—
David and Jonathan. It must have
been hard for them to say good-bye to each other.

Mike: Sure, they even cried—they were grown-up guys and they
even cried.

Tracy: I don't blame them. I moved once, and I had to say good-
bye to my best friend and go to a different school. And *I* cried.

Mike: I think I'd cry, too. You'd really have to ask God to help you
through something like that.

Tracy: Did you ever have to say good-bye to somebody special
you loved very much?

Let the puppets take it from here.

Let them tell about their best friends and times when it was
hard to say good-bye to a special friend.

A Bible Verse to Learn

A friend loves at all times. Proverbs 17:17

Talk to God

Thank God that He is one Friend who will never, never, never
leave you, no matter what. He'll be with you always, and you'll
never have to say good-bye to Him. Or if you do have a friend you
have to say good-bye to, tell God about it. He really cares, and
He'll help you find new friends if you ask Him.

Can You Find This Story in the Bible?

Find 1 Samuel 20:1-42.

147

A Chance to Get Even

Suppose someone was planning to harm you. And suppose you had a chance to TRAP HIM—get rid of him forever so that he would never never bother you again. What would you do?

David had a chance like that. Let's see what he did.

King Saul and his soldiers chased David all over the countryside. Over mountains and valleys and cities and towns. There was hardly a place anywhere in the kingdom where King Saul did not chase David. It took all of David's wits to keep one step ahead of the king.

As David was running, he kept collecting followers—more and more followers—and MORE followers. Until he had quite a little army of his own. Every time they found a place safe enough to stop and rest awhile to get their breath—they did just that. It was in one of these "safe places" where this story happened.

David led his men to a place called "Wild Goat's Rocks" in the wilderness of En Gedi.

They hid in a huge cave—way, way back in the darkness. They were talking in low tones when—

Suddenly—

En Gedi is one of the places where David hid from Saul. There are lots of caves in this area. Some are near the ground, but many are high up in the hills. Can you picture David standing on the ledge, waving to Saul down below? (Photo © Frances Blankenbaker)

They heard someone outside the cave. "SHHHH, quiet—don't move!" said David. And they all watched the entrance to the cave.

Then they saw—a man—coming in. It was King Saul himself! He had come in to the cave for a rest-stop! David watched, motionless, hardly daring to breathe as King Saul groped his way in. He took off his outer cloak. And he laid it on the ground and sat down. David's men all motioned to him in the darkness. "Now is the time," they said. "Get Saul—now, now!"

And David crawled forward, inch by inch, hardly making a sound. He could have slit King Saul's throat.

Closer.

And closer. Then David pulled a short knife from his belt and very carefully—VERY carefully—

Took hold of the bottom of Saul's cloak—

And sliced off a piece.

Then he backed away quietly, quietly and—in the darkness King Saul groped for his cloak and picked it up and felt his way back out of the cave into the light.

"But you didn't kill him," David's men whispered, louder now. "You just cut off a piece of his cloak."

"I couldn't," David whispered, but louder now. "I could not kill a king God has chosen to rule over His people. It's a sin." They waited in silence. They all knew that David was right. They waited until they were sure Saul was out away from the cave. Then David scrambled to his feet and went outside. And there he stood, waving the piece of King Saul's cloak in the air.

"M' Lord, the king," he cried.

King Saul whirled around and saw David. His jaw dropped open.

Then they just stood there staring at each other. David waved the piece of King Saul's cloak in the air. "Do you know what I have in my hand?" he cried. "Your cloak. Yes, I was back there in the cave, and I could have killed you."

Saul just stood there, his knees shaking.

"But I did NOT kill you," David said. "I told my men it was a serious SIN to attack God's chosen king."

And so they stood there. Saul the king looked like a tired old man.

And David the shepherd boy looked like a KING.

150

Tracy and Mike Talk It Over

Mike: Can you imagine that? David had a chance to kill that wicked, wicked Saul. After all, Saul tried more than once to kill David.

Tracy: I know it. And David wouldn't kill him because he was a man God had chosen to be king. What if you knew somebody who had been mean, mean, MEAN to you for a long, long time. And then you had a chance to get even. What would you do?

Mike: If I had a chance to get even? I can tell you what I'd LIKE to do. POW! WHAM! BAM!!! But I guess I wouldn't do it. What would you do?

Let your puppets take over from here.

Help them tell about times they felt like getting even with someone. Then ask them what they should do instead of trying to get even.

Some Bible Verses to Learn

Do not repay anyone evil for evil. Romans 12:17
Do not be overcome by evil, but overcome evil with good.
Romans 12:21

Talk to God

If you ever wanted to get even with somebody who had been mean to you—tell God about it. He understands how you feel. Thank Him, too, because He takes care of things like that in His own way. He understands how you feel and He wants you to be honest with Him.

Can You Find This Story in the Bible?

Find 1 Samuel 24:1-22.

The Mystery of the Disappearing Prophet

Nobody could stop him! He went through the palace courtyards and strode up the palace steps, right past the guards before they realized it. Then up the corridors, into the huge hall and UP to the throne where the king was sitting!

He didn't fall on his face, either, the way other people did when they encountered the king. He stood up straight, a huge, stern man, dressed in a coarse camel skin garment, gathered in at the waist with a wide leather belt. And he looked the king right in the eye and said with a loud voice, "As the God of Israel lives before whom I stand, there shall not be dew nor rain these years except according to my word."

There was a shocked silence in that great room. The king opened his mouth—and closed it again. When he had gathered his wits, he leaned forward in his seat, his face a mask of rage.

"How DARE you?"

But that's as far as he got. The man had turned on his heels and disappeared in the crowd, leaving behind him a shocked silence. No one could quite believe what he had just heard.

Phew!

Who was this king and who was this man?

Well, the king was King Ahab, who was ruling God's people at this time. And his rule was a very wicked one. Under his rule, the whole country worshiped the idol Baal. The people had quite forgotten God.

And who was this man? Well, he was the great prophet Elijah, who had NOT forgotten God.

So we have a king with great armies,
and 450 prophets of Baal on his side—
And one lone prophet who had GOD on HIS side.
Soooo—you can see right off, who's going to win!
Anyhow, the strangest part of all this is that—
it DIDN'T rain!

At first no one thought much about it, but as weeks, then months and months went by without rain, a terrible fear began to fill the hearts of the people. There wasn't even any dew in the mornings to moisten the earth. And the trees and grass withered and died. And the crops? Most of them didn't even come up, and those that had got started, died or bore no fruit. People tightened their belts and began to hope for next year. Surely, things would be better next year!

But they weren't better. The ground was so hard and dry, you could take a clod of it in your hand and crumple it into dry powder. It was useless to plant seeds. In most places you couldn't even get a plow into the ground. And it tells us in God's Word—that the land was TROUBLED, and there was much suffering.

King Ahab hunted and hunted for Elijah—But he was nowhere to be found.

What the king didn't know was that, way back in the wilderness, far, far from any town or city, where deep springs still fed little streams—was Elijah.

Safe and sound! For God sent ravens (ravens are big strong black birds) every morning and every evening with meat and bread to feed Elijah. Never once in the years of famine did Elijah go hungry. There he lived alone with God.

And from there he went on to have many adventures.*

But always Elijah was waiting for the three years to be up— waiting for God to tell him when to go back and face the wicked King Ahab.

And finally that day came. The Bible tell us that the Lord spoke to Elijah and said, "Go show yourself to Ahab. I will bring rain upon the face of the earth."

WHAT?!?

And Elijah got himself up and prepared to go.

WHAT?!?

Go back and face Ahab? Ahab with his huge armies and 450 prophets of Baal on his side? And Elijah with only God on his side? Why, Ahab could have Elijah killed right on the spot! Would God be on time? And how?

What do YOU think?

---

*You can read about them in the *Great Heroes of the Bible* series by Ethel Barrett.

Tracy and Mike Talk It Over

Tracy: I think Elijah was the bravest man in all the world.

Mike: I think so, too. He's a lot braver than I would be—or you either, I betcha.

Tracy: Are there things you have to be brave about now? You don't have to face a king, but is there anybody else you're afraid to face?

Mike: You mean like maybe some kids at school who don't believe in God? Am I afraid to face them?

Tracy: Yes, that's what I mean. Be honest now.

Mike: Okay, then sometimes I am afraid when I get to thinking about it. Especially if the guy is bigger than I am.

Tracy: Okay, you were honest with me, so I'll be honest with you. Sometimes, I'm afraid, too.

Mike: But God says we shouldn't be.

Tracy: Maybe it gets easier the more you practice it.

Mike: My dad says it does. And he's not afraid of anybody.

Tracy: Can you think of somebody special you're afraid of right now? I mean afraid to talk to them about God.

Let your puppets take it from here.

(Parent/teacher: If your children can't think of a situation like this, you might share an experience you have had—and tell how God helped you.)

A Bible Verse to Learn

God said: *Do not be afraid, for I am with you.* Genesis 26:24

Talk to God

Thank God that He trusts you to tell other people about Jesus. Ask Him to help you do it. He will if you ask Him. He really cares about you.

Can You Find This Story in the Bible?

Find 1 Kings 17:1-6; 18:1

The Great Contest

When Elijah finally came face to face with the wicked King Ahab—Ahab EXPLODED!

"Is it you, O troubler of Israel?"

Elijah looked him right in the eyeballs. "I have not troubled Israel, it is YOU who has troubled Israel. You have turned away from God. And you have turned your PEOPLE away from God to worship idols."

"You—You—YOU!" Ahab sputtered.

But Elijah went right on speaking. "Now therefore, gather all the people—and the 450 prophets of Baal. Have them all go up to Mount Carmel. It is THERE that I shall answer your questions, King Ahab."

So—Ahab was the king. But Elijah was in authority—he had GOD behind him. And the KING obeyed the prophet.

Yes, sir—the proclamation was sent out all over the country and the people gathered—even the prophets of Baal—and they went up to the top of Mount Carmel. The greatest showdown in history was about to take place.

The air was tense with excitement. The people were silent as the prophet Elijah held up his hands. "How long?" he thundered.

157

"How long will you dilly-dally between two opinions? If the God of Israel be God, FOLLOW HIM. If Baal be God, FOLLOW HIM." Elijah lifted his hands again.

"I, only I, am left as a prophet of God. There are 450 prophets of Baal—450 prophets—of an idol!

No answer. Silence. Elijah raised his hands again. "Bring us two bullocks for sacrifice. Let the prophets of Baal cut up one and lay it on the wood on their altar. But make no fire. Now when you are finished, I will cut up the other and lay it on wood, and make no fire. Then you call on the name of your god, Baal, and I will call upon the name of the Lord, and the God who answers by sending down fire—HE IS GOD!"

And so the great contest started. The prophets of Baal prepared their animal and laid the pieces on the wood. And then they began to cry out to Baal.

"Answer us, O Baal, answer us!" All morning long they marched around the altar, calling, calling: "Answer us, O Baal, answer us!"

At noon Elijah began to mock them. "Shout louder," he said, "for Baal is your god. Perhaps he is busy!" The prophets' shouts grew into shrieks and Elijah kept on, "Perhaps Baal has gone on a journey and he won't hear you at all. Or perhaps he's taking a nap and needs to be awakened!"

The prophets worked themselves up into a frenzy. They slashed themselves with swords and spears so that the blood gushed forth—on and on until noon—past noon—into the hot afternoon—under the merciless sun. Why, their idol Baal, they believed, was the god of the sun—he HAD to answer. But there was no answer. It was late afternoon now and still there was no answer.

Then Elijah spoke. "Come near to me," he cried, and the crowd, weary and hot, came nearer and watched him in silence. He took some stones and repaired an old altar of the Lord that had been torn down. Then he did a strange thing. He dug a ditch

This is how the Carmel mountain range looks today. Can you picture the contest between Elijah and the prophets of Baal as it took place at the top of Mt. Carmel hundreds of years ago? (Photo © Stacey Martin)

around the altar. He commanded the people to fill four huge jars with water and pour it on the sacrifice and on the wood.*

They did as he told them, in shocked silence.

But before they could get over their shock, Elijah commanded, "Do it a second time." And everyone watched in silence as some men poured more water on. And then Elijah said, "Do it a third time." This time the water ran off the altar and filled the ditch that had been dug around the edge! It splashed and gurgled as they watched and listened, hearts beating faster.

Then Elijah looked up into heaven and began to talk to God.

"O Lord, let these people know that YOU are God in Israel and turn their hearts back to you again."

And then—

FIRE!

Yes! The fire of the Lord fell, and burned up the offering and

_____

*The water was probably hoisted up there from the Mediterranean Sea.

the wood and the stone and the dust and licked up the water that was in the ditch! And the people fell on their faces and said, "The Lord, He is God—The Lord, He is God!"

Elijah looked at Ahab. "Well, get up," he said. "Eat and drink—for already I hear the sound of rain."

But the contest was not over yet.

Would the rain come? Would it?

Tracy and Mike Talk It Over

Mike: There—you see? Elijah wasn't afraid to go back and tell all the people about God. And he told everybody BEFORE God sent the fire.

Tracy: And he knew just what to say. I'll bet he had a lot of practice.

Mike: I'll tell you what. You practice on me, and I'll practice on you.

Tracy: Practice on what? WE'RE not going to call down fire.

Mike: No! I mean practice telling people about God.

Let your puppets take it from here.

The following verses might help you tell people about the Lord God and His Son Jesus: Psalm 96:4,5; John 3:16; 1 John 4:14; John 1:12.

You might also let your puppets read Psalm 115:3-8 to find the difference between our great God and the idols some people worship. Mike can read one verse, Tracy the next and so on.

A Bible Verse to Learn

Blessed . . . are those who hear the word of God and obey it. Luke 11:28

Talk to God

Ask God to help you talk to people about Jesus. Thank Him for trusting you to do this very important job. It's one of the most important things you can do for Him.

Can You Find This Story in the Bible?

Find 1 Kings 18:16-41.

Would God Send Rain?

Well, WOULD God send the rain?

     Ahab went off to get something to eat. But Elijah went even higher on the mountain. He crouched to the ground. And began to pray. "Go to the edge," he told his servant, "and look toward the sea. Keep your eyes open for CLOUDS."

The servant went to look.

No clouds.

Elijah sent him back again.

And again.

And AGAIN!

Seven times!

And then—

The servant came BOUNCING back!

A cloud! Only as big as a man's hand—but—a cloud! A real RAIN cloud!!!

Elijah looked up, his face triumphant, "Go tell Ahab to harness up his horses and get into his chariot and hurry down from the mountainside before the rain overtakes him!"

Already the wind was blowing Elijah's hair and whipping his robes about him.

Ahab hurried into his chariot
and gave the order,
"Back home to Jezreel!"
That was down the valley.
And then—
The RAIN! It came down in torrents. Children danced in it,
splashed in it—people held their faces up to it—folks who had
never spoken to each other before hugged each other and danced
for joy! It seemed as though the earth itself would cry out in
thanksgiving and praise! But the strangest sight of all was—Elijah.
He had tucked his long robes up into his belt and was running—
RUNNING—ahead of Ahab's chariot.

And he ran—yes, he did! All the way down the mountainside to Jezreel!

For the Spirit of the Lord was upon him!

The contest had been won! Most of the people had turned back to God. But had AHAB'S heart been turned back to God? What do you think? We shall see in another story.

Tracy and Mike Talk It Over

Mike: Ha, Ha! and Ho, ho, ho! Good old Elijah! He didn't give up.

He could have quit after God sent the fire.

Tracy: Yes, but his prayer was only half answered, and he didn't quit. He kept right on praying.

Mike: Have you ever quit when a prayer was half answered? Did you give up after that?

Tracy: Yes. I guess I have, lots of times. But I shouldn't.

Mike: That's right, we shouldn't. We should keep right on praying until the prayer is all answered. And God says, "That's it—now you can stop."

Tracy: When did you ever quit praying before God was finished answering? Can you think of a time?

Let your puppets take it from here.

A Bible Verse to Learn

Be joyful always; pray continually. 1 Thessalonians 5:16,17

Talk to God

Thank God for every prayer that He has answered for you. And ask His forgiveness for any time that you have quit too soon. Ask Him to help you keep on praying—and trusting Him to answer in the way and at the time He knows is best.

Can You Find This Story in the Bible?

Find 1 Kings 18:41-46.

Who Is
Your Hero?

Did you ever have a hero? You know, somebody you looked up to and thought about all the time and wished you could be like him? There was a young man like this in the Bible and his hero was, of all people—the great prophet Elijah. The young man's name was very much like Elijah's name—

It was ELISHA.

Now Elisha followed every bit of news about Elijah, and he listened to Elijah from a distance every chance he could get. I don't know for sure, but he may even have been with that crowd upon Mount Carmel when Elijah called down the fire and the rain. Elisha must have thought a thousand times *if only I could be like Elijah.* Of course, he never dreamed it would happen.

And then—one day—

It started out just like any other day.

Elisha was plowing a field on his father's farm. If he had seen the figure coming toward him from a distance, he would have dropped in his tracks. For this was a mountain of a man with a wide leather belt and a sleeveless outer garment over the rest of his clothes (it was called a mantle). He was walking with huge strides,

165

as if he were *going* someplace. He strode right up to Elisha, who did not see him until he was right up close, and then he stopped. Elisha looked up and just stood there, shocked, for he found himself staring into the face of—ELIJAH! Elisha stood there absolutely dumbgoozled, unable to say a word. And then the great prophet took—off—his—mantle—and—

THREW IT OVER ELISHA'S SHOULDERS!!

Now a prophet's mantle was his symbol of AUTHORITY. And if he transferred it to someone else, he was transferring the authority that went with it.

Elisha just stood there trembling and tongue-tied, and before you could say, "This is INCREDIBLE"—Elijah turned on his heels and walked away. It could mean only one thing—

Elisha had been chosen to be the next great prophet in Israel! He stood there for a minute and then his knees got unlocked, he ran full speed ahead after Elijah.

"Wait!" he gasped. "Wait! I'll go back and tell my father and mother and then I'll come with you!"

The great prophet turned to him. "Do as you wish," he said, "the decision is yours." And he strode away.

Well! Elisha ran back to tell his parents, and they told their neighbors and friends, and there was a great celebration on their farm that night.

In the days that followed, Elisha's dream of years at last became a reality. Now he was not just DREAMING of his hero, he was WALKING with him, and LIVING with him.

And learning, ever learning, from this great prophet who had chosen him to be his successor. They travelled together, and lived together and had adventures together—too many to tell here.*

Then finally the great day came—the day when Elijah would be taken away.

They were walking through a field, when Elijah suddenly turned to Elisha. "What wish shall I grant you before I'm taken away?" Elijah said.

Well, Elisha knew what he wanted more than anything else in the world. "Please grant me a double portion of your great power and your closeness to God!" he cried.

Read more about it in *The Disappearing Prophets* by Ethel Barrett.

"You have asked a hard thing," Elijah said. "BUT. If you see
me when I'm taken from you, then you will get your request."
Then suddenly—
Elisha felt a great rush of power in the air.
   Then he saw it.
      A CHARIOT OF FIRE
         PULLED BY HORSES OF FIRE!
      They SWOOOSHED down—
         right between Elisha and Elijah.
         And the next moment Elijah was
            SWEPT UP TO HEAVEN
               IN A WHIRLWIND!!!

And then everything was quiet. No chariot. No horses. And no Elijah. Quiet, quiet. Elisha was alone without his hero.

From now on, HE was the great prophet in Israel!

Tracy and Mike Talk It Over

Mike: What a way to go to heaven!!! Boy! God can do things any way He wants to, can't He?

Tracy: Just look at what He did for Elijah! A whirlwind! Wow! Elijah was a hero all right.

Mike: Do you have a hero?

Tracy: Right now my hero is Elijah.

Mike: But I mean today.

Tracy: My Sunday School teacher is sorta my hero.

Mike: My Little League coach is pretty swell. And of course, my dad.

Tracy: Let's think of some other people who'd make good heroes. I mean right now. Today. And my mom says a hero isn't always just a hero just because he's popular or famous. He's somebody you can look UP to.

Let your puppets take it from here.
Choose for your heroes people who love and obey Jesus.

A Bible Verse to Learn

Follow my example, as I follow the example of Christ.
1 Corinthians 11:1

(Paul, a follower of Jesus, said this to the people who looked up to him as a hero and an example.)

Talk to God

Thank God for giving us heroes. Ask Him to help you follow the example of the "heroes" He has put in your life.

Can You Find This Story in the Bible?

Find 2 Kings 2:9-11.

Can Elisha Fill His Hero's Shoes?

Well, Elijah was gone. Now Elisha was the prophet in Israel. Elisha traveled up and down the land, performing miracles through God, and his fame spread far and wide.

Now in the village of Shunem, there lived a man and his wife, who invited Elisha and his servant for dinner, the way you'd invite a visiting minister. And they all learned to love one another—so much that Elisha and his servant dropped in to visit this couple every time he went by their way.

"I've been thinking," the woman said to her husband one day. "It's a blessing just to have that man around our house. I wish we could do something for him, more than just having him stop by for dinner. Do you think we could fix him a room up on the roof? We could put a bed in there. And a table and a chair and an oil lamp. That's all he'd need."

And so it was done. And whenever Elisha and his servant traveled up that way, they had a place to eat and a place to sleep.

"There must be something I can do," Elisha said to his servant one night, "to show these people how much we appreciate their hospitality."

The servant thought for a moment. "A child!" he said. "The woman doesn't have a child."

"Of course," Elisha said. "That's it. Call her up here."

The servant did just that, and a moment later she was standing in the doorway of the little upper room. Elisha came right to the point.

"Next year, at about this time," he said, "you will have a son."

But she shook her head sadly. "Oh no, my lord," she said, "all my life I have wanted a son. I am weary with hoping and waiting. Please don't joke with me." And she turned away and went back downstairs.

But Elisha had meant exactly what he said. And sure enough, the prophecy to her came true. And she did have a son!

Well, the years went by and they were happy years for the woman and her husband. Their son grew into a strong, healthy boy.

And then one day in a flash, their world went crashing at their feet.

The day started out just like any other day. The boy went out to the fields to be with his father. And it was harvesttime, the hottest time of the year. It happened faster than it takes to tell it.

"My head!" The boy cried suddenly. And a moment later, he fell to the ground, moaning with pain.

His father told a servant to carry the boy back to the house. And there, his mother rocked him and soothed him and nursed him. BUT it was all in vain. In spite of all they could do, and even as she held him, he died.

And the woman did the only thing she could think of. She struggled upstairs, carrying the boy, into Elisha's room. She laid him on the prophet's bed, and then she hurried back downstairs and found her husband. "Send me a donkey and a servant," she cried. "I must go to Elisha the prophet! And hurry!"

Moments later, a donkey was saddled. "Hurry!" she said to the servant. And they were on their way to Mount Carmel to find Elisha.

When she got to him, she fell to the ground and grabbed hold of his feet. "The son you promised me is dead!" she cried.

The top photo shows a model of a Bible times home. Notice the stairs going up to the flat roof and the room that has been built on the roof. Elisha's friends built him a room like this on the roof of their house. (Photo of model at Holyland Hotel, Jerusalem, Israel, by Frances Blankenbaker.) One of the items Elisha's friends put in his room was an oil lamp like the one in the bottom photo. (Photo © Tim Howard)

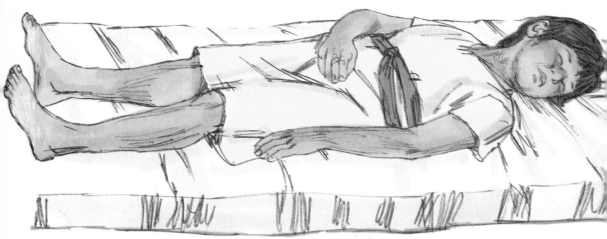

"Quick," Elisha said to his servant. "Take my staff and hurry on ahead and lay my staff on the boy's face. We'll be right behind you."

The servant ran on ahead, and Elisha and the woman followed as fast as they could. But before they even got inside of the house, the servant ran to meet them. "It's no use," he said. "I laid your staff on the child's face, but he is dead."

When they reached the house, Elisha hurried on ahead. "He's upstairs," the woman called after him. "In your room. I laid him on your cot."

Elisha ran up the stairs. The child was indeed dead.

Elisha shut the door behind him. And he began to pray. He went over to the bed and lay down on the child's body. He put his mouth on the boy's mouth and his hands on the boy's hands—

And lo and behold—the boy's body began to grow warm again!

Elisha walked back and forth in the room. Then he stretched himself again upon the body of the boy. And prayed. And then— and then—

The boy stirred. His eyelids flickered, and then—and then—

He SNEEZED! Once. Twice. Three times—four—five—six— seven times! Elisha sprang from the bed and dashed to the door and called out to his servant, "Come here! And call the woman!"

Moments later, the woman came into the room, out of breath from running up the stairs. She went over to the bed.

Her son was alive! She picked him up. And carried him slowly down the stairs and into the house, crying all the way.

Elisha stood there alone. And the power of God surged through him, and he knew again, as he'd known so many times before, that the power that had once been his hero's, was now his.

For even as God had used Elijah, He was now using him!

Tracy and Mike Talk It Over

Mike: That sure was a great story.

Tracy: I know. And just think—Elisha turned out to be just as great as Elijah ever was. God let him bring that woman's son back to life again!

Mike: And it all started when the woman and her husband invited Elisha to stay with them—and fixed him a room so he could stay anytime, as long as he wanted to.

Tracy: Maybe it's a good idea to invite people of God into your home whenever you can.

Mike: Yeah—but they might not be great people.

Tracy: Well, you don't know. Even if they're not great, we should invite them into our homes. The Bible tells us to show hospitality.

Mike: That's right. That's all hospitality means—it means inviting people into your home and being kind to them.

Tracy: My mom said that every time we talk to somebody about Jesus, and they invite Him into their lives—that's a miracle!

Mike: It sure is, oh, boy! God is in the miracle business! He even uses us kids!

Tracy: Can you think of people our parents know whom they could invite into our homes?

Mike: Well, not just people our parents know. People we know, too. Can we think of anybody right now?

Let your puppets take it from here.

A Bible Verse to Learn

Offer hospitality to one another. 1 Peter 4:9

Talk to God

Thank God for giving you chances to invite people into your home. And when the people get there, be NICE to them. Ask God to show you how to make them happy.

Can You Find This Story in the Bible?

Find 2 Kings 4:8-37.

One Against 400

Well, wouldn't you know? King Ahab's feathers were ruffled again.

There was a city called Ramoth-Gilead that really belonged to Israel. But the Syrians had gotten ahold of it. And Ahab was itching to get it back. It wasn't until Jehoshaphat, the king of Judah, came down to see him that Ahab saw his chance.

"Jehoshaphat," he said slyly, "would you go with me to fight against Ramoth-Gilead and get it back from the Syrians?"

Jehoshaphat said he would. "There's one little thing, though," he said, "Let's ask for the word of the Lord first."

The word of the Lord, good grief! Ahab worshiped idols—he wasn't on speaking terms with the Lord. But he gathered all his prophets together—there were about 400 of them—and put the question to them.

"Shall I go up to fight against Ramoth-Gilead?" he asked.

Well, they buzzed and mumbled and pulled their beards and finally—"Yes," they cried, "for the Lord surely will deliver the city into your hands."

174

But Jehoshaphat had a queasy feeling. He was pretty sure these were false prophets. "Isn't there another prophet of the Lord we could ask?" he said to Ahab. "A TRUE prophet?"

Ahab glared at him for a moment. Then he said, "There is another man we could ask. His name is Micaiah. But I hate him. He never says anything GOOD about me."

"Oh, don't say that," Jehoshaphat said quickly. "Why don't we call him and ask him, just to be sure?"

And Ahab had to call the one prophet he knew would not be a "yes" man.

When the king's officers found Micaiah, they warned him what he would be up against. "Be careful," they said. "The king's prophets have already told him to go up against Syria—that the Lord would deliver Ramoth-Gilead into his hands. So just be smart and tell them the same thing, it won't cost you anything. And who knows? Maybe he will like you again."

"I will tell him what the Lord tells me to tell him," Micaiah answered. "And I don't care whether he likes me or not."

When Micaiah faced King Ahab and King Jehoshaphat, it was plain that he meant what he said.

"All right, Micaiah," Ahab said, "do I go up against the Syrians or do I stay home? Tell me."

Micaiah bowed low in a mock bow. "Oh, by all means, go up against the Syrians in battle. You'll be sure to win."

Ahab's face turned purple with rage. Micaiah was mocking him and he knew it.

"How many times must I tell you to speak nothing but the TRUTH in the name of the Lord?" he bellowed. "How DARE you? You are mocking my prophets!"

"Yes, I'm mocking your prophets," Micaiah said, "for they are lying!"

And he glared at the prophets. And they glared back at him. One of them even stepped forward and struck him in the face.

Micaiah turned to Ahab. "You want the truth? Here then is the truth," he said, and everyone knew that this time he meant what he said.

"I saw all your soldiers scattered on the mountains like sheep without a shepherd. And the Lord said, *These soldiers have no masters, let them return to their homes.*"

Ahab sat staring at Micaiah.
He knew what that meant.
If the soldiers had no master it meant only one thing—
Micaiah was prophesying his DEATH.

"Take him away!" Ahab shouted. "Put him in prison! Feed him on bread and water until I get back from the battle—VICTORIOUS."

Ahab was shouting on the outside, but on the inside he was scared to death.

"That stupid prophet!" he said to Jehoshaphat. "I don't believe a word he said. But I'm not taking any chances. I'll go up to battle dressed like an ORDINARY soldier. You go up in your KINGLY robes. They will all know who YOU are. And as for ME, no one will know I am King Ahab. I'll fool them all!"

And so they went into the battle. And it was just as King Ahab had figured. When the Syrian soldiers started going after Jehoshaphat, he cried out to them and told them who he was. So they let him alone. It was AHAB they were after.

But no one could find Ahab. Ha! Clever!

Nobody can find me, Ahab thought and grinned a wicked grin. *Nobody even knows I'm here. Nobody knows—*

OOOOFFF!—

Some soldier in the battle had shot an arrow that had gone WHOOOOSH!—right between the joints of Ahab's armor and deep inside Ahab's body.

The one who shot the arrow didn't plan it that way. But that's the way it turned out.

"I'm wounded," Ahab moaned to his chariot driver, who steered the chariot out of the battle as quickly as he could.

Ahab's soldiers propped him up in the chariot as best they could. But in spite of all their efforts, he finally died.

And a cry went through the battlefield, "Go home, go home—all of you. The battle is over! The king is dead!"

King Ahab had been killed—in spite of his cleverness—by a stray arrow, shot without aim.

THE LORD HAD SPOKEN.

And Micaiah had stood up before 400 prophets and DARED TO SPEAK THE TRUTH!

Tracy and Mike Talk It Over

Mike: Boy! Micaiah stood before four hundred prophets and TWO KINGS!

Tracy: Could you do that?

Mike: I could if I had GOOD news for them. But if I had to tell them something they didn't want to hear, I'd be scared!

Tracy: Well, would you be brave enough to tell the truth if you knew you might get in trouble for telling the truth?

Mike: I'll have to think about that!

Tracy: Suppose you and some other kid did something wrong and the other kid said you *didn't* do it. And you knew if you told the truth you'd BOTH be in trouble?

Mike: Eeeek!

Tracy: Would you be brave enough to tell the truth then?

Mike: EEEK!

Tracy: My dad says you should tell the truth even if you make somebody angry with you.

Mike: Yeah. And even if it means you'll get punished.

Let your puppets take it from there.

It would be fun to use some "what if" stories and let your puppets tell what they would do in that situation. Like "what if you broke your brother's favorite model airplane and he says, 'Who broke this?'" or, "What if—(you finish it)."

A Bible Verse to Learn

Do not lie to each other. Colossians 3:9

Talk to God

Thank God for letting you know how *important* it is to tell the truth. Ask Him to help you to be brave and tell the truth even when it looks tough.

Can You Find This Story in the Bible?

Find 1 Kings 22:1-36.

ATTACK!!

Did you ever have to pass a test? Sometimes we have tests to see how SMART we are. And sometimes to see how BRAVE. And sometimes to see how OBEDIENT. Now most of the tests in our lives are little ones. But the boy in this story had tests that got bigger and BIGGER and harder and HARDER. The boy's name was Daniel. And he lived in the city of Jerusalem back in Bible times.

The first test came like a bolt of lightning.

Imagine being a nobleman's son and living in a beautiful house and having nothing to worry about one day, and the NEXT day— King Nebuchadnezzar of Babylon was seizing Jerusalem!

ATTACK!

Soldiers were running in the streets, searching the houses and dragging out the biggest and the smartest and the strongest boys—boys like DANIEL!!!

Yes, sir, that's just what happened. Daniel was snug and safe in his father's house in Jerusalem one day—and on his way to Babylon the next day—a captive!

Now Babylon was a HUGE city. It had high, thick walls around it. And inside, it was filled with temples for idols. And beautiful gardens. And of course many palaces for the king.

Anyhow, it was in Babylon where Daniel ran into—

THREE OF HIS CLOSEST FRIENDS!! They had been taken captive, too! So the four of them stuck close together to buck each other up and give each other strength.

And guess where they were sent? TO THE KING'S PALACE! For the king had said, "Send me some boys. I want them to be strong and healthly and very, very smart, so we can train them to help me rule my kingdom." And Daniel and his friends were very, very SMART.

So they studied along with all the other young captives who had been chosen. They had beautiful clothes. And fine teachers. And they ate in the king's dining room.

Ah HAH!

That was when the second test came. In the king's dining room. The food they were served there was food God had never allowed them to eat back in Jerusalem. For the people in Babylon worshiped IDOLS. And the food in the king's dining room had been sacrificed to these idols.

And Daniel and his friends were expected to eat the king's food and drink the king's wine!

"Auuugh!" Daniel said, "We can't eat this stuff!"

But what to do? Go to the counselor in charge of food and tell him you couldn't eat the king's food and could you have something else, like vegetables and plenty of fruit—and NO WINE? It was up to Daniel to decide which to do—eat the king's food and drink his wine—or obey God.

If he obeyed God, he might make everybody FURIOUS.

HE MIGHT EVEN LOSE HIS HEAD!

Daniel and his friends were taken to the great city of Babylon. The huge Ishtar Gate of Babylon has been rebuilt to show how it looked in Bible times. (Photo © Joyce Thimsen)

Tracy and Mike Talk It Over

Tracy: What a choice Daniel had to make! What d'you think you would have done?

Mike: Maybe I would have chosen all the goodies—I dunno—.

Tracy: All those sweets and meats do sound good.

Mike: But their meats were sacrificed to idols

Tracy: Yeah. And God told the Hebrews not to eat stuff like that. But I can't remember just why.

Mike: I know! I know! God said, "You shall have no other gods before ME!"* That's why.

Tracy: I'm glad WE don't have to worry about the food WE eat. It's not sacrificed to idols.

Mike: But we have OTHER kinds of decisions we have to make—like choosing the right kinds of programs to watch on TV.

Tracy: Yeah—I see what you mean. Can you think of any more decisions we have to make?

Have your puppets take over from here. Help them think up some "what if" situations like "what if someone offered to let you copy his homework?" Ask Mike and Tracy to tell what they would do.

A Bible Verse to Learn

I have hidden your word in my heart that I might not sin against you. Psalm 119:11

To hide God's Word in your heart means to memorize Bible verses and think about them.

Talk to God

Thank God that He cares so much about you that He wants you to love Him best. Ask Him to help you so you will know how to make the right decisions. Thank Him for giving you the Bible, that tells you what He wants you to do.

Can You Find This Story in the Bible?

Find Daniel 1:1-8.

---

*You can find this verse in Exodus 20:3.

To Eat or
Not to Eat

Yes—there was no doubt about it. Daniel and his friends were
in real trouble. They either had to eat the king's food and
drink the king's wine—or obey God. Daniel decided to obey God.

"What!?" cried the counselor. "Vegetables and fruits? And
water instead of wine? You must be out of your heads!"

"Just let us try it for ten days," said Daniel.

"But you won't be happy like the others," the counselor
groaned. "You'll be pale. And sad. And you'll look like STRING
BEANS."

But in the end he agreed. Daniel and his friends were allowed
to eat their vegetables and fruit and drink water instead of the
king's wine.

And as the days went by—

Daniel and his friends grew HEALTHIER

and HAPPIER

and ROSIER

Until the counselor finally said, "You look G-R-E-A-T!"

And it was true. God gave Daniel and his friends such wisdom
and understanding and skill that they breezed through their training
with no trouble at all. And they were found to be TEN TIMES

BETTER than all the wise men of the kingdom! And they were put in positions of importance as ADVISORS TO THE KING!

Now while all this was going on, the king had been building a HUGE statue outside the city. It was as tall as an eight-story building! And when it was finished, the king had it covered all over with pure gold! So when it shone in the sun it could be seen for miles and miles!

And that's when the NEXT test came.

Now Daniel had gone off to another part of the kingdom on official business. So the test did not come for HIM. This test came for his THREE FRIENDS!

It came on the great day when all the people gathered to celebrate the completion of the statue. Daniel's friends didn't know what the king would do. Suppose he ordered them to BOW DOWN to that statue?!?

HORRORS!!!!

Whatever would they do? Daniel was their leader and he was GONE.

WOULD THEY BE ABLE TO PASS
THE TEST WITHOUT HIM???!
WAIT AND SEE!

Tracy and Mike Talk It Over

Mike: What are they going to do **now?**
They're alone without Daniel.
They don't have a leader.

Tracy: No—and they don't have their parents either. What do you
suppose the king will ask them to do? Maybe they'll have to
choose whether to obey the king or obey God!

Mike: But they practiced obeying when they chose to eat the right
food. Maybe all that practicing will make them stronger.

Tracy: Do you suppose when you practice on little things you get
stronger when **big** things come along?

Mike: I'll bet you do.

Tracy: Can you think of little things in your life when you obeyed?
Did you get stronger for **bigger** things? And did you obey
when there was nobody around to ask?

Have your puppets take it from here.
Help them tell about times when they obeyed in little things—
and times they obeyed when there was no older person around.

A Bible Verse to Learn

Whoever can be trusted with very little can also be trusted with much.
Luke 16:10

Talk to God

Ask God to help you when you are on your own and have to make
a choice. He really cares! And when you make the right choice
when your parents or your teacher aren't around to help you—it
makes you STRONG.

Can You Find This Story in the Bible?

Find Daniel 1:8-20; 3:1-3.

Walking Through the Fire

Such excitement! The whole city of Babylon was in an uproar! For the great day had finally come to honor the king's statue—the great golden idol!

Everybody was there! The princes and governors of all the land! A great platform had been built—way up high—a place for the king and all the important people to sit. And off to the side was a furnace—a HUGE furnace. A great fire had been built inside of it—and the flames leapt out of its door and shot up into the air.

Daniel's three friends stood on the edge of the crowd. They looked at each other. Somebody was going to get ROASTED, they thought. But WHY? And for WHAT?

Then the king's messenger stepped forward to make an announcement. The crowd grew quiet, to listen.

"When the music starts to play," the messenger shouted, "everyone shall fall—flat on the ground—and worship the great statue!"

What? WHAT?!!!? Fall down and worship an IDOL?!?

"And whoever does not obey," the messenger went on, "will be thrown into the FIERY FURNACE!"

Daniel's three friends looked at one another. The hairs on their heads began to prickle.

And then—

The music started with a great blast. And there was a swoooosh! as everyone fell forward, flat on the ground!

All except Daniel's three friends. They stood there, straight and tall. Their hairs were still prickling, but they had made up their minds to pass the test!

Moments later they were grabbed by rough soldiers and hustled up to the king.

"WHAT?" the king cried, his face purple with rage. "You refuse to bow down to my idol? Well, then, you'll be thrown into the furnace. And what God will deliver you then?"

"Our God," they said looking him right in the eyeballs.

"And if He doesn't?" The king's eyes were boggling out of his head by now. He was FURIOUS!!!

"Even if He doesn't," they answered, "we will STILL not worship your idol."

The next thing they knew they were bound hand and foot and—POPPED INTO THE FIERY FURNACE!!!

But wait!

What was THIS? It didn't even feel HOT in there!

And their hands and feet were no longer tied!

And—and—there was somebody standing beside them.

It was—it was—THE LORD!

Everybody saw it. The soldiers had popped in three people and now there were four! And they were walking around, cool as a breeze, and not on fire at all!

The king rushed toward the furnace. "Come out!" he cried, "COME OOUUTT!"

And Daniel's three friends walked out, as nicely as you please, cool as cucumbers—and their hair was not even singed! They did not even SMELL SMOKEY!!

They had passed the test. THEY HAD PASSED THE TEST!

Tracy and Mike Talk It Over

Mike: I don't see how they could be so brave!

Tracy: I checked that out with my mom. And she said sometimes we're not brave at all until we **have** to be. Then all of a sudden God gives us the strength to do what we have to do.

Mike: Just think! They passed the test when Daniel wasn't even there. Could you do that?

Tracy: Nobody ever tried to toss me into a fiery furnace. So I don't know what you mean.

Mike: I mean it's easier to be brave when you have a strong leader right close by. Can you think of any times when you had to be brave when nobody was around to buck you up?

Have your puppets take it from here.

A Bible Verse to Learn

The LORD is with me; I will not be afraid. Psalm 118:6

Talk to God

Thank God that He is always with you even when it doesn't SEEM like it. Ask Him to protect you in everything you do today.

Can You Find This Story in the Bible?

Find Daniel 3:1-30.

Throw Him to the Lions!

As the years went by, Babylon had a new king. And THIS king was a GOOD king. Daniel became more powerful and MORE powerful. Until he was one of the most powerful rulers in the land! You wouldn't think anything BAD could possibly happen to Daniel NOW.

But WAIT. What was THIS?!?

All the other officials became JEALOUS of Daniel. They became SO jealous that they went to the king with what seemed like a WONDERFUL idea. "O king," they said, "let's give all the people a rest. You can pass a law that nobody can worship any God for THIRTY DAYS. And anyone who does not obey will be thrown to the LIONS!"

Why, OF COURSE—the king thought there would be no harm in passing that law. Give everybody a rest. And, of course, everybody would be happy to obey.

BUT HE FORGOT ABOUT DANIEL!

When the news got around, Daniel knew this was going to be the HARDEST test he would ever have to take. But he also knew what he had to do. The next morning he went to his window and knelt and prayed to God.

And everybody saw him.

And at noon he went to his window and prayed.

189

And everybody saw him.

And in the evening he went to his window and prayed.

AND EVERYBODY SAW HIM.

AND THE KING COULD NOT GO BACK ON HIS LAW!!!

A few days later, all the people and a very sad king gathered around and watched as the soldiers tied a rope around Daniel and lowered him down

down

DOWN

into the lions' den.

Daniel stood down there as they rolled the huge stone over the top.

It was dark, dark, PITCH BLACK.

Daniel could hear the lions as they circled around him, closer and closer and CLOSER.

And then he saw something else.

A strange light.

It got BRIGHTER and BRIGHTER and BRIGHTER.

IT WAS AN ANGEL!!!

STANDING BETWEEN HIM AND THE LIONS!

All night long the lions cowered in a corner.

And they never dared to come near Daniel!

Finally it was morning. And the soldiers removed the stone.

They tugged—upp! and Pulled—oops! and the light streamed down from above. And Daniel heard the king's voice. "Daniel! Daniel! Has God been able to save you from the lions?"

"Yes!" Daniel called back, "God sent His angel to shut the lions' mouths—they couldn't come near me!"

The king was beside himself with joy. "Lift him out!" he cried. "Quickly!"

And they did. What a cheer rose in the air! Daniel was alive! And everyone knew that GOD had saved him!

And Daniel was still the most important person in the kingdom.

But there was something more important to Daniel.

He had passed the test. HE HAD PASSED THE TEST!

Tracy and Mike Talk It Over

Tracy: Daniel asked for that. Getting thrown in the lions' den. He **asked** for it! Why?

Mike: Maybe he was so used to standing up for something he thought was right, he just kept on praying in spite of everything.

Tracy: Do you know what I think? I think he'd had so much practice obeying God that he KNEW God could protect him.

Mike: I think so, too. But that sure takes a lot of practice.

Tracy: What can we practice up on today? There must be some things.

Have your puppets take it from here.

A Bible Verse to Learn

The Lord is my helper; I will not be afraid. Hebrews 13:6

Talk to God

Thank God for sending you tests to practice on, so you'll get stronger and stronger. Ask Him to help you not to be afraid.

Can You Find This Story in the Bible?

Find Daniel 6:1-28.

A Little Orphan Becomes a Queen

This is a story that's full of surprises. They all happen to a girl who had been carried off from Jerusalem to Persia as a captive Jew.

Her name was Esther.

She was not only a captive, but she was also an orphan. And the only family she had was her older cousin Mordecai, who had adopted her. Now Mordecai was a gatekeeper at the king's court. It was not a job of great power and Mordecai and Esther lived a very ordinary life. Until—one day—

An announcement decree went forth from the palace—King Ahasuerus was searching for a new queen! The most beautiful girls in the land were being sought, to be brought to the palace so the king could choose his queen from among them! And Mordecai took Esther to the palace. And she was chosen to stay there to be dusted and polished and made ready to stand before the king. And lo and behold, the king chose HER for his queen!

Well, that was a big enough surprise to hold Mordecai and Esther for a while. Everything went smoothly at the palace and they kept in touch with each other and Mordecai reported to

Esther lived in Persia as a captive Jew at the time Xerxes was king. These columns are all that are left of the Entrance Hall and porch of the palace where King Xerxes lived hundreds of years ago. The entrance is guarded by carvings of huge winged bulls. (Photo © Joyce Thimsen)

193

Esther the bits of news he heard at the gate. Most of it was not important. But one day, Mordecai overheard something that made his hair stand up.

Two of the guards were plotting to KILL the king!

Mordecai got word to Esther—

Esther got word to the king—

The guards were caught and punished—

And the whole thing was written up in the king's record book!

And do you know what happened? Do you know what happened?

Absolutely nothing!

The record book was put away on a shelf where it gathered dust and was FORGOTTEN.

And that would have been the end of it—except for one thing.

God had a plan for Esther's life.

He had a REASON for making Esther queen.

And there were more
surprises ahead!

Tracy and Mike Talk It Over

Tracy: Just think! Esther went from being a poor little orphan—to being a QUEEN!

Mike: Yeah—That was great, all right. But Esther and Mordecai saved the king's life. And after it was written in the king's record book, everbody forgot about it!

Tracy: Esther and Mordecai never got any credit!

Mike: They didn't get a reward!

Tracy: They probably didn't even get a THANK YOU!

Mike: What if YOU did something great. Wouldn't you want a reward?

Tracy: Yeah—I guess it would be nice if people made a fuss over it. But I never did anything great enough.

Mike: Well, even SORTA great. You wouldn't want people to just FORGET about it. Would you?

Tracy: I guess God wants us to do good deeds even if we never get thanked.

Mike: Or even if people forget about it.

Tracy: One thing is for sure. GOD won't forget about it. Can you think of something GOOD that you did and nobody noticed or said thanks?

Have you puppets take it from here.

A Bible Verse to Learn

Whatever you do, work at it with all your heart, as working for the Lord. Colossians 3:23

Talk to God

Thank God that He sees every good thing you do, even if nobody else says thank you. Ask Him to help you do right even if nobody else notices.

Can You Find This Story in the Bible?

Find Esther 2:1-23.

The Queen's Life in Danger

The next surprise in Esther's life was a HORRIBLE ONE.

There was a certain nobleman in the king's court whose name was Haman. He was POWERFUL—next in power to the king himself. Why, every time he came and went through the gates, all the guards bowed to him as if they were worshiping a divine being. But Mordecai bowed to no one but God. Haman did not notice this at first (he probably had his nose too high up in the air), but when the other servants at the gate told him, he was FURIOUS.

"What? *What!?*" "Who is this fellow? How dare he?" "What? He's a Jew?" "Did you say a *Jew?*" And the more Haman thought about it, the angrier he became. So Mordecai was a Jew, was he? Well he could be destroyed. No, that was not enough. *All* the Jews should be destroyed. Aha! that was better. Haman decided to go to the king.

Which he did. He went to the king and told him that there were certain people in the kingdom who were not keeping the king's laws. Would the king give an order that they be destroyed? And the king said he would. What's more, he gave Haman permission to write the decree. And WHAT'S MORE he gave Haman his official

signet ring to seal the deal. He knew that trusty Haman would take care of everything. BUT. What he did NOT know was—

Haman was talking about the Jewish captives—THOUSANDS OF THEM! And what's more, his faithful Mordecai at the gate was a captive Jew, and what's MORE—his beautiful queen Esther was also a Jew!

HORRORS! All the Jews in the kingdom were to be destroyed!

Now the surprises came heaping upon Esther's head, one after the other. First came the word that Uncle Mordecai was outside. He had dressed himself in sackcloth and sprinkled ashes upon his head. Then next, a messenger delivered a copy of Haman's decree, and a personal message from Uncle Mordecai:

GO TO THE KING AND BEG HIM FOR
THE LIFE OF YOUR PEOPLE!

Esther sank down on a couch, her knees had turned to jelly. Why no one could go to the king without an invitation. NO ONE. Not even his QUEEN. Anyone who dared go into that inner court would be sentenced to death—unless the king held out his scepter.

"Go to Mordecai," Esther told her messengers, "and remind him of this."

The messengers hurried off. But Esther was telling her Uncle Mordecai what he already knew. The message he shot back to Esther was a scolding. "Why do you suppose you were chosen queen?" it said. "Who knows? Perhaps it was for this very reason—so that you could save your people."

At first such a stern answer from Uncle Mordecai knocked the wind out of Esther. But not for long. She took a deep breath, stood up straight—and sent this message back to Mordecai: "Send the word out, Uncle Mordecai. Tell the Jewish people not to eat or drink for three days. Tell them to pray. And my maids and I will stay here and pray. And we won't eat a crumb or drink a drop."

Well! One day went by—

Two days—

Three—

Then a very very frightened Esther walked slowly toward the court of the king. She walked toward the throne like a person in a dream—closer—closer—

What would the next surprise be?

She shuddered to think of it.

Tracy and Mike Talk It Over

Mike: Boy. That sure was a horrible surprise for Esther.

Tracy: Yes, it sure was. But she did the right thing, all right. She took her problem to God.

Mike: What if you had a horrible problem in your own life? Not as horrible as Esther's, but anyway, to you it might seem horrible. What would you do?

Tracy: Well, I would have to take my problem to God.

Mike: I would, too, but first I'd take it to my parents and ask them what to do. Just like Esther took her problem to Mordecai. Then she took it to God. But she knew that Mordecai was praying for her all the while.

Tracy: Well, I would take it to my parents, too, but I'll betcha they would tell me I should take it to God, and then we'd all take it to God together, I'll betcha.

Mike: Can you think of any time you had a problem like this, and you took it to your parents and then you all took it to God?

Tracy: Well, I can't think of one right off.

Mike: Well, can you think of any of your friends who did? Or can you think of ANYBODY who did?

Let your puppets take it from here.

A Bible Verse to Learn

In everything, by prayer . . . present your requests to God.
Philippians 4:6

Talk to God

Thank God that He cares about all your problems. Ask Him to forgive you for any times you have not taken your problems to Him. And if you can think of any problem you have right now, tell Him about it. Tell Him ALL about it, every little bit, and trust Him to take care of it for you.

Can You Find This Story in the Bible?

Find Esther 3:1-15; 4:1-17; 5:1.

A Strange Dinner Party

Esther stood before the king, trembling. What would he say? What would he DO? According to the law of the kingdom, he could have her killed!

But instead—

He held out his scepter!

Phew!

"What is your wish, Queen Esther, and what is your request? It shall be given you, even to half the kingdom."

Esther could barely speak, the surprise was so great. "If it please the king," she stammered, "let the king—and Haman—come this day to the dinner that I have prepared for them."

And the king said yes!

Phew! So far so good! And sure enough, that night at dinner, the king had not forgotten!

"What is your request?" the king asked Esther again.

"If it please the king," Esther said, "let the king and Haman come again tomorrow night and dine with me. Then I'll tell you my request." And the king agreed.

Now exactly why Esther did that—postponed her request for another day—we can't be sure. Could it be that there were a few more surprises on the way that hadn't happened yet? Could it be that God WANTED Esther to wait another day? Let's read on and see.

Haman left the palace that night so proud he was floating.
His feet hardly touched the ground.

But when he got to the gate, there was Mordecai. And
Mordecai did not bow! Haman sputtered to himself all the way
home. His wife and friends were waiting to hear the news of the
evening.

"I dined with the king and queen tonight, and I'm invited to dine
with them tomorrow night," he told his wife and friends.

"How jolly," they said, clapping. "Be happy," they cried.

"I CAN'T be happy, as long as I see Mordecai the Jew sitting
there at the king's gate," he bellowed, and his face turned purple
and they thought any moment smoke would come out of his ears.

"You don't have to put up with that," they said. "Have a gallows
made. Speak to the king. Have Mordecai hanged. Then go dine
with the king with a merry heart."

"Why, that is a jolly idea," he cried. "I'll give the orders at once
to have the gallows made and I'll get that wretched Mordecai out of
my hair forever."

Haman did exactly that.

BUT . . .

Something ELSE was going on that night.

Do you remember that book of records that never got read to the king? Well, that book of records was the beginning of one of the biggest surprises of all. Wait and see.

Tracy and Mike Talk It Over

Mike: Phew! Esther got in to see the king all right—but that wicked Haman!

Tracy: I know! And he did it all because he hated Mordecai—and because he wanted to be important.

Mike: It was pretty sneaky, wasn't it?

Tracy: Did you ever do anything sneaky because you didn't like somebody, or because you wanted to feel important?

Mike: I never did anything as bad as that.

Tracy: But did you ever do anything even just a little bit sneaky, because you wanted to be important, or because you didn't like somebody?

Mike: We-e-l-l-l—

Tracy: Okay, did you ever THINK about it, maybe even just a little bit?

Let your puppets take it from here.

A Bible Verse to Learn

Do nothing out of selfish ambition . . . but in humility consider others better than yourselves. Philippians 2:3

Talk to God

It's great to be important. God understands this. But if you've ever even thought about doing something sneaky to be important, tell God about it. He understands this, too. Ask Him to forgive you. Ask Him to help you not to do anything sneaky about it. And remember that to Him you will ALWAYS be important. Thank Him for this and leave your problem with Him. He will work it out.

Can You Find This Story in the Bible?

Find Esther 5:1-14.

God Always Keeps His Promises

A HA!
    God was still in charge!

For that very night the king could not sleep. And he ordered—of all things—that book of records to be read to him. His secretary read on—and on—and ON.

When suddenly—What was this? Mordecai saved the king's life?

WHAT? Has anything been done to honor him?

No?

What?

Nothing???

By this time, it was daylight.

"Who's outside standing in the court?" the king asked.

"Haman," they said.

And sure enough, he was. He'd come to ask the king to have Mordecai hanged.

"Tell him to come in," said the king.

They did.

"Tell me, Haman," said the king. "What shall be done to the man whom the king wishes to honor?"

Naturally Haman thought HE was the one whom the king wanted to honor. And naturally he thought up a dinger.

"Let royal clothes be brought which the king has worn. Yes, and the horse the king has ridden. And a royal crown set upon his head. Then let one of the royal princes conduct him on horseback through the open square of the city. And shout before him, "This is the man the king delights to honor!" Haman was so puffed up with pride by now he nearly burst.

"Good," said the king. "Do this to Mordecai the Jew and make haste."

MORDECAI? GOOD GRIEF!

Well, poor Haman did as he was told, but it was the worst day of his life.

And he still had a dinner party ahead!

It was a very nervous Haman who sat at the queen's table that night. He could hardly get his mind on what was being said. His scalp prickled.

"What is your request?" the king was saying to Esther.

"If it please the king," Esther said, "let my life be saved and the lives of my people. This cruel decree has ordered them all to be killed, and there are thousands of us here living in Persia."

"US?" asked the king.

"Yes, oh King, for I am a Jew."

Haman nearly slid off his couch. Esther a Jew? What a horrible development!

"And who is he, and where is he who dares to do this thing?" the king was saying.

"An enemy," said Esther. "The man who sits at this table— Haman."

The jig was up!

There was a long silence. Then one of the servants suddenly found his tongue. "Oh, King," he said, "there's a gallows standing by the house of Prince Haman. The gallows that he had made for Mordecai—the man who saved your life."

The king nodded his head toward Haman without even looking at him. "Hang him on it," he said.

The jig *was* up.

All the mischief that wicked Haman had planned came back on his own head, or in this case, around his neck.

204

The king could not cancel his decree, but he could issue
ANOTHER decree, and he did. His new decree stated that all the
Jews could defend themselves. Which meant they would be fighting
under the king's protection. Which meant that nobody dared to
attack them.

So instead of a great slaughter—there was a great
CELEBRATION. All the Jews in the land celebrated with a great
feast to thank God and express their joy. That feast is held among
the Jews to this very day. It's called the Feast of Purim.

And Mordecai? Mordecai was given Haman's old position as
one of the most powerful princes of the land.

Esther knew now why she had been made Queen of Persia at
this particular time—to save her people!

Tracy and Mike Talk It Over

Mike: Wow! Wow, wow, wow! Woooooooeeeee! God sure had everything worked out, didn't He?

Tracy: Yes, He had it all worked out because Esther took her problem to Him. But I can't help feeling sorry for poor Haman.

Mike: Well I don't feel sorry for what happened to him, but I do feel sorry that he didn't take HIS problem to God.

Tracy: I know. If poor Haman had taken his problem to God—

Mike: But he didn't.

Tracy: He didn't because he was full of hate and he wanted to be important. That's bad.

Mike: Did you ever think that maybe you were born just when you were born—for a special reason?

Tracy: My mom told me that I was. That I was born for a special reason—and that God would tell me just what it is.

Mike: Well, my dad told me the same thing. I know that I was born for a special purpose.

Tracy: Can you think of what it might be? Can you think of anything? Anything at all? Can you think of what you might want to do when you grow up?

Let your puppets take it from here.

A Bible Verse to Learn

The Lord will fulfill His purpose for me. Psalm 138:8

Talk to God

Thank God for protecting the Jewish people. Thank Him for always keeping His promises. And ask Him to help you to remember the times He has kept promises He made to YOU. Thank Him that you have been born for a reason. And that He has a plan for your life.

Can You Find This Story in the Bible?

Find Esther, chapters 7-10.

The Greatest Promise in the World

GIFT! It's one of the nicest words in the world.

Roll it around in your mind. Just THINKING about it can make you happy. Or you can roll it around on your tongue, and just SAYING it can make you happy.

Now a gift doesn't do anybody any good if it just SITS there. Somebody has to GIVE it, and then somebody has to GET it. So the first thing we think when we hear the word gift is—Who gave it? And who GOT it?

Can you imagine a gift so great and so important that it changed the whole world? Well there was a gift just that important. Who gave it? God. Who can get it? The world. The whole world means us, you and me.

Whatever could it be?

It wasn't a palace.

It wasn't gold.

It was—a baby.

A very special baby—God's own son, the baby Jesus.

It was promised to a young woman named Mary. And to a kind man named Joseph. And this is how it all happened.

Mary and Joseph lived in Bible times when angels sometimes spoke to people. One day Mary was praying to God. She didn't know there was going to be a gift. She didn't expect an angel. She didn't even expect a PROMISE. But suddenly—

An angel! Right there before her eyes!

Mary was frightened. She'd never SEEN an angel before. And this angel was SPEAKING to her.

"Don't be afraid, Mary," the angel said. "God loves you very much. And He has this to say to you. You're going to be the mother of a baby boy. He'll be God's own son. And His name will be Jesus."

And then the angel was gone—just like that!

Mary stopped in her tracks. This was a most wonderful promise. And when God makes a promise, He always keeps it. God had actually said this. This would be the greatest gift in all the world.

Then one night while Joseph was sleeping, he saw an angel, too. And the angel told him all about Mary and all about what was going to happen. Oh, joy!

I am going to be the mother of a baby boy, Mary thought, and she made some blankets to keep Him warm. *He will be God's Son,* she thought, and she made clothes for Him to wear. *His name will be Jesus,* she thought, and she fixed a bed for Him to sleep in.

So Mary and Joseph got ready for this wonderful gift, for they knew it was coming. They had seen an angel and God had promised it. It was going to be the greatest gift in all the world.

Tracy and Mike Talk it Over

Tracy: I sure wish I'd been there when Mary saw the angel. Imagine seeing an angel!

Mike: Yeah—imagine looking at an angel with your own eyeballs!

Tracy: An angel **talking** to you!

Mike: Hey! Wait a minute. Maybe we have something even better!

Tracy: How could anything be better than **that**?

Mike: Well, we have God's promises in writing! So we can read them any time we want.

209

Tracy: Show me. Where is the angel's promise to Mary?

Mike: Right here in the Bible, see! The angel said "Do not be afraid, Mary, you . . . will . . . give birth to a son, . . . He . . . will be called the Son of the Most High" (Luke 1:30,32). See? Anytime I need to remember that promise I can look it up.

Some Bible Promises to Think About for Today

Genesis 28:15	Isaiah 41:10
Jeremiah 33:3	Romans 8:28
Psalm 121:3	Philippians 4:19

Pick one of the promises above. What are some times when that promise can help you today? What do you think Tracy and Mike would say about times when that promise would help them? Use your puppets to talk about it.

A Bible Verse to Learn

Not one word has failed of all the good promises he [God] *gave.*
1 Kings 8:56

Talk to God

Thank God for His promises to YOU.

Can You Find This Story in the Bible?

Find Luke 1:26-38; Matthew 1:18-25.

The Promise
Comes True

Well, now, God had made Mary and Joseph an earth-shaking promise. He promised them a very special baby—God's own son, the baby Jesus.

Imagine!

You'd think that Mary should go to the very best hospital or maybe even a king's palace for this very special baby to be born. Or maybe stay home and have servants and nurses hurrying and scurrying about, carrying trays and orange juice and sheets and medicine and bumping into each other, with maids to comb her hair and bathe the new baby and dress Him in the finest clothing and brush what little hair He had up to a curl on top and carry Him to Mary's bedside and put Him gently alongside her with His tiny head snuggled in the finest of pillows—

But none of this happened at all.

What really happened is quite amazing.

It all began with a king's order. The Bible tells us "In those days Caesar Augustus issued a decree that a census should be taken of the entire Roman world . . . . And everyone went to his own town to register" (Luke 2:1,3).

What was this? Everyone to his own city? Why Joseph's home town was BETHLEHEM! Which meant that Joseph and Mary had to pack up a few belongings on a little donkey and leave their comfortable little house in Nazareth and clump along bumpy roads—all the way to Bethlehem to pay their taxes and sign the king's book.

First there was the matter of crowds. When they finally got to Bethlehem it was SPILLING OVER with people who had also come to pay their taxes. People and donkeys and camels and bundles and food and sheep and goats—what a traffic jam! You just can't IMAGINE the confusion.

And then there was the matter of a place to stay and that was the WORST part, for there was NO place to stay. All the inns were filled*. The inns were filled. EVERY place that had rooms to rent was filled. And poor Mary and Joseph went all over Bethlehem,

---

*An inn is like a motel, only instead of having cars, the people had donkeys or camels to park out in a stable.

knocking on doors and getting turned away until—

One innkeeper said, "Wait." He had just thought of something, and what he thought of was not nice beds and clean sheets and a warm bath. It was a STABLE—where the cattle slept, and that is where Mary and Joseph finally went. And that was where, that very night, God kept His promise—and the baby Jesus was born. And instead of servants and nurses and doctors—there were donkeys and sheep and cows sleeping.

Yes, there the baby Jesus was born, and there Mary wrapped Him in soft clean cloth and laid Him—oh so carefully—in one of the troughs where the hay was kept for the animals to eat. It was called a manger.

It might SEEM that everything had gone wrong. But actually everything had gone exactly as God wanted it to go.

God had kept His promise—the baby Jesus was here.

Tracy and Mike Talk it Over

Tracy: Do you think Jesus should have been born in a palace?
Mike: Maybe that would mean that God gave His great gift only to rich people.
Tracy: So if Jesus was born in a manger—that means God's gift was for the richest down to the poorest.
Mike: And that means *everybody*.
Tracy: Wow! That means US!

Have your puppets tell each other about their favorite Christmas gift—and compare it with God's gift.

A Bible Verse to Learn

He [God] *loved us and sent his Son.* 1 John 4:10

Talk to God

In your own words, thank God for His gift.

Can You Find This Story in the Bible?

Find Luke 2:1-7.

The Strangest Announcement in the World

When Jesus was born, there were no announcement cards sent out. But people found out about it in the strangest ways!

There were some people who lived nearby who found out about it. They were shepherds. And they found out about it in the middle of the night. And this is how it happened.

They were watching their sheep on a hillside. Everything was so quiet you could hear a blade of grass if it twittered in the breeze. Once in awhile, a baby lamb would wake up and go "Baaaaa"—but its mother would lick its ears and say "Shhhhhhhh"—and it would go back to sleep. Then everything would be quiet again. Then suddenly—

There was an ANGEL—right before their eyes! And a bright, BRIGHT light—right in the sky!

The shepherds couldn't believe their eyes. They looked at the angel. And at the bright light. And at each other. And they were afraid.

"Don't be afraid," the angel said. "I have good news! A Saviour* has just been born. He is in Bethlehem right this minute. Lying in a manger."

---

*The Saviour is the Lord Jesus.

Sheep still graze on the hillsides outside the city of Bethlehem. Think about what happened here on the night Jesus was born. Can you picture the shepherds and sheep as they were startled by a bright light—and as they heard the angel's message and then saw the sky filled with angels praising God? (Photo © Stacey Martin)

"The Saviour! Oh joy! Could it be TRUE?"

Just then the sky was FULL of angels. And they were saying, "Glory to God in the highest, and on earth peace, good will toward men."

And then, suddenly—

The angels were gone.

And the bright light was gone.

And it was dark again.

The shepherds looked at each other. It MUST be true! They would GO to Bethlehem and find out. And they DID.

They stumbled across the fields and puffed up the hills and sneaked through the streets. And then—

They came to a stable. They looked in the doorway. And there was Mary. There was Joseph. There were sheep. And goats. And cows. There was a manger with hay in it. And there—all snuggled in the hay—was baby Jesus!

It was true!

Shhh. They went in quietly. And shhh. They knelt down. And shhh. They thanked God for baby Jesus.

And then they went back to their sheep.

Oh, they were happy! For they had found out about the most important baby that had ever been born. Not by telephone. Not by an announcement card. Not by a letter. But by ANGELS—and a light in the sky!

For this was not just any baby. This was God's Son.

Tracy and Mike Talk it Over

Mike: That sure was a strange way to make an announcement.

Tracy: Well it was the most important thing that ever happened. So it took a special announcement.

Mike: God can still use angels today to tell everybody the good news about Jesus. Well, can't He?

Tracy: Of COURSE He can.

Mike: It would sure be exciting if He did.

Tracy: But instead of using angels, look what God does! He chooses us to tell the good news!

Mike: Wow! Us.

Have your puppets tell the news about Jesus as we would do it today.

A Bible Verse to Learn

Today in the town of David [Bethlehem] *a Savior has been born to you; he is Christ the Lord.* Luke 2:11

Talk to God

Ask God to help you think of more ways you can tell others about Jesus.

Can You Find This Story in the Bible?

Find Luke 2:8-20.

Two Dreams that Saved a Little Child

People found out about the birth of Jesus in strange ways. There were people who lived nearby who found out about it. They were shepherds. And there were people who lived far away who found out about it. They were wise men who lived in another country. And when THEY found out about it, they did something that nearly caused baby Jesus harm—DREADFUL harm. It happened this way.

These wise men studied the stars. They knew that God had promised to send a Saviour-King.* One night they saw a HUGE star, brighter than all the rest. And they knew it must be the star that would tell them where the Saviour-King was.

So they packed some gifts and got on their camels and followed that star right to Jerusalem. And they went straight to the palace where King Herod lived.

"We have followed God's star," they told King Herod.

"We are looking for the new King God promised."

King Herod was very polite and asked them all about the star.

"The child is not here," said King Herod. "But when you find Him, let me know where He is. I would like to worship Him, too." And he sent them on their way to Bethlehem.

---

*This was baby Jesus.

The wise men went on to look for Jesus. But they didn't know one thing—

Herod was a WICKED king. And he didn't want to find Jesus to WORSHIP Him. He wanted to KILL Jesus!

When the wise men came to where Mary and Joseph and little Jesus were, they unpacked their camels and brought out the finest gifts of gold and rare perfumes. And they knelt down and worshiped Jesus. Then they got ready to go back and tell the wicked king where Jesus was. And they would have told him, and Jesus might have been KILLED—except for one thing.

God was watching!

That night in a dream, God told the wise men, "Do not go back to wicked King Herod. He doesn't want to worship Jesus. He wants to have Him KILLED. Go back to your own country."

And the wise men did!

But King Herod was angry. He called his soldiers. "Go to Bethlehem," he told them, "and find this child—I want to have Him killed!"

But God was still watching!

At night, in a dream, God told Joseph to take Mary and Jesus and run away. Mary and Joseph packed up their things and wrapped up little Jesus. They quietly left the city and went across the desert until they got to Egypt, a country far away.

And when the soldiers got to Bethlehem and looked in all the places where there were little children so they could kill baby Jesus—He was gone!

King Herod never found Jesus. And Mary and Joseph didn't bring Him back until the wicked king was dead.

No harm could come to God's Son. Because God was watching!

Tracy and Mike Talk it Over

Mike: Phew! *That* was close, all right!

Tracy: They didn't have telegrams back in those days to warn people—

Mike: No hot-lines either. No radios—

Tracy: And no emergency number like 911!

Mike: So God used dreams! How about that?

Tracy: Can you think of a time when God saved you from danger?

Mike: Or times when He watches over us even when we're NOT in danger. At school. Or when we're traveling. And even at home.

Tracy: Tell me about times God took care of YOU. And I'll tell you about times God took care of ME.

Use your puppets to talk about times when God takes care of you and saves you from danger.

A Bible Verse to Learn

The Lord watches over you. Psalm 121:5.

Talk to God

Thank God in your own words for watching over you and keeping you from harm.

Can You Find This Story in the Bible?

Find Matthew 2:1-23.

When Jesus Was a Little Boy

Even though Jesus was God's own son, He had to grow up just like any other little boy. And God was watching over Him every minute.

After the wicked King Herod was dead, and Mary and Joseph and Jesus came back from Egypt—they went to Nazareth to live. Nazareth wasn't a great big city with tall buildings and temples and lots of traffic. It was a little country town tucked away in the hills.

The Bible tells us that Jesus had to learn things. And that He obeyed His mother and Joseph. So we have a pretty good idea of what Jesus' life was like.

In the morning, the sunshine would sneak in Jesus' window and across His bedroom floor and up the side of His bed and over the top of His covers—and in His eyes—and wake Him. Mary would pour water in a basin and help Jesus get washed and dressed. And then it was time for breakfast.

While Mary got breakfast, Jesus would put the dishes on the low bench they used for a table and spread the mats on the floor for them to sit on. Then Mary and Joseph and Jesus sat around on the mats and Joseph would thank God for their breakfast while they all bowed their heads. Then they would eat barley cakes with fresh

butter and honey. And while they ate, they would talk about what they were going to do that day and ask God to help them do everything just right.

There were so many things to do INSIDE their house.

And Jesus helped with everything. He helped feed the animals. He helped Mary get water at the well. And He helped Joseph, too.

He helped Joseph in his carpenter shop. He handed Joseph nails and pieces of wood. He caught the curly shavings as they fell to the floor. And He watched the sawdust sprinkle the floor, like snow, when Joseph went szhhh-szhhh with the saw. And Jesus obeyed Mary and Joseph in everything they asked Him to do.

There were so many things to do OUTSIDE their house.

There were walks in the hills and rides on the donkey, and picnics, and friends to play with.

And in the evening Mary and Joseph and Jesus would sit on their doorstep and watch the sun go down—and talk about God. They would tell God's stories over and over, until Jesus knew them all by heart.

And then Jesus would say His prayers and go to bed. And the stars came out—and all of Nazareth would go to sleep, tucked away there in the hills.

That's the way the other people in Nazareth lived. And that's the way Jesus lived, too.

Even though He was God's Son, He had to grow up just like any other little boy.

And God was watching over Him every minute.

Tracy and Mike Talk It Over

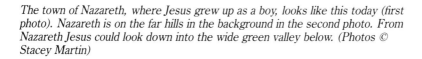

Mike: Boy, Jesus sure had a lot of work to do.

Tracy: Both inside the house and outside the house. Do you do all these things inside and outside?

The town of Nazareth, where Jesus grew up as a boy, looks like this today (first photo). Nazareth is on the far hills in the background in the second photo. From Nazareth Jesus could look down into the wide green valley below. (Photos © Stacey Martin)

223

Mike: W-e-e-l-l-l, I don't have a donkey.

Tracy: Do you have a dog?

Mike: I have a dog and two cats.

Tracy: And I'll bet you begged your parents to let you have them.

Mike: Yeah—I do remember that. I begged them.

Tracy: And did you promise your parents you'd take care of them?

Mike: Yeah—I sure did.

Tracy: And did you keep your promise?

Mike: Well, sort of. But it got to be a bother after a while, emptying cat boxes and cleaning up after the dog. And I got busier and busier with other things. You know how it is.

Tracy: And who takes care of them the most?

Mike: Well, my mother does, but she's not too happy about it. What about you, Tracy? Do you do all your chores because you *like* to?

Tracy: No, I do all my chores because my parents *make* me.

Mike: And do you like this?

Tracy: No, I don't like it a bit, but I suppose it's good training.

Mike: It sure was good training for Jesus.

Have your puppets talk about their chores . . . what they like and what they don't like.

A Bible Verse to Learn

Children, obey your parents in the Lord, for this is right.
Ephesians 6:1

Talk to God

In your own words, tell God about the chores you have to do that you don't like. He already knows that whatever you're asked to do, whether you like it or not, is good training. But be honest with Him. He likes that. And He'll help you.

Can You Find This Story in the Bible?

Find Luke 2:40,52.

When Jesus Was a Big Boy

Remember the very first day Mother took you to school? She marched you into the building and up the hall, right into Miss Chalk-dust's room. She introduced you to your teacher and whispered something in your ear about using your handkerchief instead of your sleeve—and then she went HOME—and you were on your own! Oh, joy, oh, HORRORS! You were half-glad and half-scared. It was all so new! And then, after a while, you got used to it. Remember?

Well, Jesus had to go to school, too. While He was busy helping Mary and Joseph, and learning to obey—he was GROWING. And before He knew it, it was time for Him to start going to school.

NOW, things were different. In the morning, when the first rays of the sun s-t-r-e-t-c-h-e-d across His bedcovers and got to His face to wake Him, it was more important to get up than ever before.

School!

Jesus washed and dressed Himself. Mary didn't help Him with these things any more. Jesus spent some time by Himself, talking alone with His heavenly Father.

The chores had to be done quickly now. Jesus fed His pets and

set the table—and now that He was bigger, perhaps Joseph let HIM thank God for their breakfast!

There wasn't any Miss Chalk-dust, and school wasn't a big building with lots of rooms and desks. The teacher was the MINISTER, and school was in the SYNAGOGUE*. And everything was different. Jesus had to get used to it, the same as you had to get used to your school. He sat on the floor, cross-legged, along with the other boys, and learned.

Jesus learned God's Word. He learned to read from a long strip of paper with a stick at each end. He u-n-r-o-l-l-e-d it and read it, and rolled it up again on the other stick. It was called a scroll.

Jesus listened to everything the teacher said, and then said it over and OVER until He knew it by heart. There was so much to learn!

Some things were easy. Some things were hard, and Jesus bowed His head and asked God to help Him.

And when He got home, He told Mary all the new things He had learned.

And when Mary and Joseph sat on their doorstep in the evening, to watch the sun go down, sometimes Joseph let HIM tell the Bible story.

Oh, yes, things were different now.

Everything was more exciting. Everything was more important. Even though Jesus was God's own Son, He went to school and LEARNED things. Just like any other boy!

Tracy and Mike Talk it Over

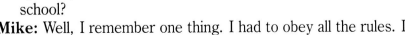

Tracy: Mike, do you remember all the dumb things you did when you were just a little kid?

Mike: Well, my mother tells me that I dumped my cereal over my head, but I can't remember.

Tracy: Do you remember what it was like when you first went to school?

Mike: Well, I remember one thing. I had to obey all the rules. I

---

*A synagogue is a place of worship just as your church is.

227

never heard of so many rules and I had to obey them all. But it really wasn't so hard.

Tracy: Why?

Mike: Well, I learned about rules and how I should obey them. My parents taught me before I ever went to school. WOW!

Tracy: What do you mean, "Wow"?

Mike: Well, I learned that I would always have somebody I had to obey, like my teachers and my coach when I got into Little League baseball. There was always SOMEBODY telling me what to do.

Tracy: Me, too. What about Sunday School?

Mike: I learned that you don't run through the church or run up and down the halls and you don't throw paper airplanes or tie two guys' shoelaces together. But I learned a lot about God.

Tracy: I did, too, because my parents taught me. We talked about God every night before we went to bed, and every night they taught me something.

Mike: Boy, doesn't that make you feel old? It sure does me.

Tracy: Me, too. But I think we still have a lot more to learn. We haven't learned half of it yet.

Have your puppets tell each other what they've learned.

A Bible Verse to Learn

I will not neglect your word. Psalm 119:16

Talk to God

In your own words tell God what you think you've learned. And maybe you should remember to thank Him for it.

Can You Find This Story in the Bible?

Find Luke 2:40,46,47,52.

Lost:
One Boy

Jesus could hardly wait until He was twelve years old. Because when He was twelve years old, something VERY IMPORTANT was going to happen. He was going to go with Mary and Joseph to the big Temple in Jerusalem! Every year, fathers and mothers traveled to the big Temple to worship—but boys couldn't go to the Temple services until they were twelve.

All His life, Jesus thought about the wonderful day when He would be allowed to go. And at last He was twelve!

Oh, joy! Such scrubbing and packing and cooking to get ready! What a golden day it was, when Mary and Joseph and Jesus started out, with their little donkey packed right up to his long ears. What fun to meet other families along the way and travel along together. There were donkeys and camels and carts to carry things and people. There were goats and sheep and turtledoves and cattle to give to God. There were days of traveling. And finally—

JERUSALEM!

Jerusalem—with its funny, crooked cobblestone streets and rows of stores right outdoors. And the TEMPLE!

They could see its golden roof from a distance. They went through its big gates and into the huge courts. Of course, they could not go into the INNER courts. They could not see the rich curtains of red and blue and purple—and the altar and table and candlesticks made of gold. But they went each day to worship God. And at last it was time to go back to Nazareth.

Mary and Joseph thought Jesus was with them when they started across the hills with the crowd. But when they stopped in the evening to rest, they looked for Him—and He was GONE!

How dreadful! They went through the crowds, asking everybody. Nobody had seen Jesus. Mary and Joseph went back to Jerusalem again, and for three days they looked in the streets, in the homes of their friends—everywhere. Then they looked in the Temple —

And there He was!

Not playing. Not crying. But sitting with the wise men of the Temple, talking about the things of God! Jesus was answering the questions of the wise men, and the men were surprised at how much He knew.

"Why have you done this, my son?" Mary asked Him. "We've been looking for you everywhere."

"You didn't look in the right place," said Jesus. "Didn't you know I'd be here about my Father's business?"

They went back home to Nazareth, and the days went on exactly as they had before.

But Jesus had given Mary and Joseph quite a jolt.

He reminded them of WHO HE WAS.

They never forgot that day, when Jesus

was twelve years old. And they never forgot that Jesus is really God's own Son.

Tracy and Mike Talk It Over

Mike: Wow! I'm glad the Bible tells about when Jesus was a boy.

Tracy: Me, too. We can do some of the same things Jesus did when He was a boy.

Mike: What do you mean? WE can't go to the Temple like Jesus did.

Tracy: No, but we can go to our church building. It doesn't look like the Temple did—but we can go there and learn about God. The Temple was the "house of the Lord"—the place for worshiping God—and so is our church building.

Mike: Yeah! I see what you mean—we can go there to worship God and learn about Him.

Tracy: Jesus really liked going to the Temple. I wonder what was His favorite thing to do there.

Mike: I don't know—but my favorite thing to do in the worship service is sing to God—I like to sing!

Tracy: My favorite thing is learning Bible verses—I can say a lot of verses now.

Have your puppets tell their favorite things to do when they go to "the house of the Lord."

A Bible Verse to Learn

I rejoiced with those who said to me, "Let us go to the house of the LORD." Psalm 122:1

Talk to God

In your own words, thank God that He let us know Jesus when He was a baby and when He was a boy. And thank Him for this because it helps us to understand Him better, and especially because He understands us. Thank God, too, that you can worship Him in the "house of the Lord"—just as Jesus did.

Can You Find This Story in the Bible?

Find Luke 2:40-52.

231

The Children Find a Friend

The day the wonderful news came, the little town by the lake was turned upside down with excitement, and nothing was ever quite the same again. The news was—well it was so exciting that it spread like wildfire!

The children heard it in the streets, and they ran into their houses, falling over pet lambs and sending pigeons flying in every direction.

"Mother! Jesus is here!"

And their mothers stopped mixing the bread dough and said, "Jesus? Where?"

"Here, Mother. HERE. He's on His way to Jerusalem, and He's stopping here and He has His helpers with Him, and—"

But their mothers had already rinsed their hands and dried them on their aprons.

"Jesus is here!" they cried. "Go get your father!"

And so the news spread, until everybody knew about it, and the fishing was forgotten and the shops were closed. Everybody wanted to see Jesus. The mothers especially wanted Jesus to bless their children.

Perhaps if they hurried and got there early, they could see Him. The children stuck close to their mothers, and they all talked at once as they hurried to the place where Jesus was.

But when they got there, the most DREADFUL of all things happened. They couldn't even get near Jesus!

The mothers tried to get through the crowd. The children tried to squiggle through. But they couldn't.

The mothers thought perhaps if they spoke to Jesus' disciples, THEN they could see Him. "Please—" they began, "we wondered if perhaps—"

"What do you want here?" the disciples said. Well, that wasn't a very good beginning. But the mothers grew bolder.

"We want Jesus to bless our children!" they cried. And the disciples said, "Go away. Jesus isn't interested in children."

Well, that was that. The mothers and children turned sadly away. It was no use. But then—That WASN'T that!

"Don't turn the children away," said a voice. Who was that? Who was THAT? They listened hard. "Bring them here to me," the voice went on. It was JESUS! Oh, joy!

Could it be true?

It WAS! The crowd was separating to let them through!

The children started to walk toward Jesus, slowly. Then they walked faster. Then they RAN. They ran right up to Him and stood around Jesus, by His knee— and He put His hand on their heads and blessed them. Oh, it was wonderful. It was better than they had dared dream!

They all went home happy. And on evenings when they sat in their doorways, they had something to talk about for YEARS.

The little town was never quite the same again. Jesus had stopped there.

The fathers and mothers were never quite the same again. For they had SEEN Him.

And the children were never quite the same again. For they had TOUCHED Him!

Tracy and Mike Talk it Over

Mike: Well, I sure understood Jesus as a baby and as a little boy and even as a big boy, but now He's a man. I just don't understand grown-ups at all. Jesus—a man?!?

Tracy: Well, you might not understand Him—but He understands YOU. You just heard that in the story.

Mike: Yeah—He sure cared about children then, but I still have a question. I want to know if He cares about children NOW.

Tracy: Well, He sure does, dummy. Don't we read about it in the Bible? He cares about everybody, and that includes us. When He says He cares about everybody—He means EVERYBODY.

Mike: Well, I sure hope so. I'd hate to think that He left us out.

Tracy: Oh, Mike, you dummy. Just think of all the ways Jesus cares about children.

Have your puppets tell each other about all the ways they can think of that show that Jesus does care about children.

A Bible Verse to Learn

We love because he first loved us. 1 John 4:19

Talk to God

Why don't you thank God for every single thing you can remember that shows you that Jesus does care about you, then ask Him to help you remember some ways that He showed you He does care about you—that you may have forgotten. So many things God does for you that you don't even know about. Why don't you thank Him?

Can You Find This Story in the Bible?

Find Matthew 19:13-15; Mark 10:13-16; Luke 18:15-17.

The Boy the Doctors Couldn't Cure

The beautiful house in Capernaum was quiet. The nobleman who lived there was brokenhearted. His little boy was very, very sick.

"There is nothing we can do for him," said the doctors. And they shook their heads.

"Nothing to do—nothing to do—", thought the nobleman, as he stood by his son's bed. "Nothing, unless—"

Then he suddenly thought of something! Jesus was in the town of Cana! The nobleman had heard his friends telling wonderful tales of how Jesus was teaching, and curing the sick—

CURING THE SICK!

"Get my horse ready," the nobleman said to his servants. "I'm going to Cana!"

The servants hurried to obey, and as the nobleman left, he said, "Take care of my son. I'm going to bring Jesus back with me!" And off he went to Cana as fast as he could go.

It was about one o'clock when the nobleman got to Cana. When he saw the crowds, his heart sank. *Jesus will be too busy to come,* he thought, as he pushed his way through the crowd. *He won't be able to come, and my son will die,* he thought, as he struggled to get up close to where Jesus was. By the time he got to Jesus, the nobleman was almost crying.

"Please, Jesus!" he said. "Come to Capernaum and heal my son!"

Jesus looked at the nobleman, with the kindest eyes in the world. Jesus didn't say He would come. He didn't say He WOULDN'T come. He said something far more wonderful. He simply said, "Go back home. Your son is better."

And suddenly, in his heart, the nobleman KNEW that his son was better. Jesus had told him so! He thanked Jesus, and went back through the crowds, and started for home. All his fear was gone. He knew Jesus meant what He said.

All the way home he thought about it. And as he got near his house—

Servants from his house—running to meet him! "Your son did not die!" they cried. "He is well!"

"I know—I know!" said the nobleman. "Jesus healed him!" And they all started back for the house.

"Just when," asked the nobleman on the way back to the house, "did my son start to get better?"

"About one o'clock," they cried. "Yes—it was just one o'clock."

"Ahhh," he said quietly, "that is just what I expected you to say. For that is just the hour Jesus said to me, 'Go back home—your son is better.'"

The large group of trees on the shore of the Sea of Galilee marks the place where the city of Capernaum stood in Bible times. Ruins of a synagogue and some houses have been found here. The nobleman whose son Jesus healed lived in this city. (Photo © Gil Beers)

237

And they bowed their heads then and there and thanked God.

And oh—the house in Capernaum was bright again! And the nobleman was happy. Jesus had healed his son without even seeing him. Nobody else could do that.

But Jesus could! He is the Son of God.

Tracy and Mike Talk it Over

Mike: Heyyy—Wait just a minute! My eyeballs can't see what I'm supposed to be believing! Are you telling me that Jesus could heal that nobleman's son by long distance?

Tracy: Well, Jesus did just that. And when the nobleman got home, his son was cured.

Mike: Yes, I know that's true. But what about doctors?

Tracy: Well, we have doctors to help make us well, but who do you suppose helps the doctors?

Mike: Well, God does, of course. I know that, dummy.

Tracy: So all right, I'm a dummy. But do you think that Jesus can heal people when sometimes the doctors can't?

Mike: Well, He sure did that time.

Tracy: Do you think that maybe sometimes He still does it now?

Mike: Well, it would have to be a miracle.

Tracy: Well, do you think miracles still happen today?

Mike: I'm not so sure. It makes my eyeballs come clear out of my head to even think about it.

Have your puppets discuss this.

(Parent/teacher: Help children know that God is the same today as He was in Bible times. He has all power and wisdom. Nothing is too hard for Him. He answers our prayers in the way He knows is best.)

A Bible Verse to Learn

Jesus healed many who had various diseases. Mark 1:34

Can You Find This Story in the Bible?

Find John 4:46-53.

The Man Who Went Through the Roof

The poor man had been sick for years and years. There wasn't a doctor in the world who could heal him. He couldn't even move. Other people had to care for him. Every day was just like every other day. Nothing ever happened.

And then—

one day—

the whole town was all astir. Up one street and down another, people were passing the word along. Jesus was in town!

The friends of the sick man thought, "How wonderful it would be if Jesus would make this poor man well." Then they got busy.

They tied a rope to each corner of his mat-bed so they could carry him. They—hup!—lifted him up and started off to find Jesus. And then they ran into—

TROUBLE.

Jesus wasn't in the market square. He was in a HOUSE—and the crowd was so great they couldn't get in. The men squiggled and they squaggled to try to get through the crowd. No use. They asked people to let them through. Nobody budged. There they stood, with their poor sick friend on his mat-bed, without a chance of ever getting in. There was nothing they could do—nothing—

WAIT A MINUTE!

There WAS something they could do! It was daring. It was RISKY. But they decided to do it anyhow. They worked their way to the side of the house—to the outside stairs that led up to the roof. And—hup!—up they went, mat-bed and all. The men—

oops—made their way carefully across the roof. They made an opening in the roof—and THEN—

They carefully, c-a-r-e-f-u-l-l-y let the sick man down—
d-o-w-n—

into the room.

The people in the room looked up. They could hardly believe their eyes! They reached up to grab the mat-bed and backed up to make room for it. And the next thing the poor sick man knew—he was lying right there at Jesus' feet, looking up into Jesus' kind face! And Jesus looked down at him and said, "Your sins are forgiven. Get up. Take up your mat and walk."

WALK!

Everybody waited. Jesus had told the sick man to WALK! And that's exactly what the man did. He got up with wonder and rolled up his bed with amazement, and with tear-filled eyes he thanked Jesus. Then as the crowd parted to let him through, he walked right out of that house.

His good friends came leaping down the stairs. And they all met in front of the house and laughed and cried together and probably even hugged each other! How wonderful it was! It was almost too good to be true!

The sick man was now well. And oh so HAPPY. Because Jesus, the Son of God, healed him. And because he had friends who CARED enough to BRING him to Jesus!

Tracy and Mike Talk It Over

Mike: Boy, those friends certainly went to a lot of trouble to get that man to Jesus, tearing through a roof and everything. I've always wondered about one thing, though. I wonder if these guys ever went back later and cleaned up their mess?

Tracy: Well, we'll never know. Anyhow this is today. What can we do today?

Mike: Sure we can do things today. There's a kid I know in school and every Sunday we go over and pick him up and take him to Sunday School. And he's not even in our neighborhood. My dad drives blocks and blocks and blocks out of our way to pick him up. He couldn't get to Sunday School without us.

Tracy: Well, I knew a lady once who went out of her way to take some kids to Vacation Bible School. And she had to take them on a bus. Boy, that was sure out of her way.

Mike: It sure was. Hey, can you think of kids we know that we might be able to get to Sunday School—if we go out of our way?

Let your puppets take over from here. You could wind up with a carful!

A Bible Verse to Learn

Serve one another in love. Galatians 5:13

Talk to God

Ask God to help you think of kids you might get to Sunday School if you went out of your way. Thank Him that He can use you to do some pretty great things!

Can You Find This Story in the Bible?

Find Matthew 9:1-8; Mark 2:1-12; Luke 5:17-26.

The Day Jesus Didn't Hurry

The only one who could help Jairus—was Jesus.

Hurry, hurry, hurry, thought Jairus, as he left his house. *Hurry, hurry, hurry,* he thought as he went through the streets to the lakeside. He HAD to find Jesus. And for a very important reason. His daughter was very, very sick—and if he didn't hurry, she would die.

When Jairus got to the lakeside, the crowd was so great, his heart nearly stopped beating. Would he be on time? Would Jesus come? *Hurry, hurry, hurry,* he thought, as he squeezed his way through the crowd.

Then—at last—there was Jesus!

Jairus ran up to Him and fell down at His feet and said, "Oh Jesus—my little girl is so sick she is going to die. Please come and make her well!"

And Jesus said, "Yes, I will go with you."

Oh, joy!

Jairus scrambled to his feet and began to lead the way. "Oh, hurry, hurry, hurry," sang in his mind. But the crowds were so great, they COULDN'T hurry. People pressed in on Jesus from every side. Sick people—curious people—nice people—noisy people. They pressed Him back and slowed Him down. They kept stopping Him along the way, some to talk to Him—some to just touch His robes. And Jairus thought of his daughter at home, and his mind shouted—"Hurry—HURRY!"

And then—

The worst possible thing happened.

Somebody from Jairus' house broke through the crowd and said, "It's too late! Your daughter is dead. There is no need for Jesus to come." There was no longer any need to hurry.

Jairus looked sadly at Jesus. And Jesus said softly, "Don't be afraid. Just trust me—and I'll help you." And they went on toward Jairus' house.

Jairus didn't hurry now. There was no need to hurry. But he couldn't help wondering. What was Jesus going to DO?

When they got to Jairus' house—Jairus knew the news was true, all right. The house was filled with people—crying. His daughter was dead.

Jesus looked at the people. He looked at poor Jairus. And then He took command. He took the girl's mother and Jairus. He took three of His disciples. And they all went into the girl's room. Nobody else could go in.

There was the girl lying on the bed—and she looked just as if she were sleeping. Jesus went up to her and took her hand—and said—"Little girl, arise."

Jairus held his breath. Nobody in the room made a sound. And then—and then—the girl's eyelashes fluttered.

She began to breathe.

She sat up and looked around.

Then she STOOD UP!

There she was, standing before them—alive, and completely well again!

The only one who could have helped her—was Jesus. And it didn't matter whether He hurried or not. Jesus could do anything. He is the Son of God.

Tracy and Mike Talk It Over

Mike: Boy, Jesus sure took His time in answering that prayer.

Tracy: I know. And He sure takes His time in answering some of my prayers today.

Mike: I know. Mine, too. Sometimes I wish He'd be more in a hurry. Why do you suppose He waits so long sometimes?

Tracy: Well, I asked my dad about that once and he said it's to teach us to be patient and to trust Him.

Mike: Well, I trust Him all right, but I can't always be patient.

Tracy: Hey—I asked my Sunday School teacher about this one time and he said that God has four ways of answering prayer: sometimes He says yes, and sometimes He says no, sometimes He says wait, and sometimes He says, Here's something better.

Mike: Well, the important thing is that God knows what He's doing. Can you think of some times you've asked God to answer a prayer? Which way did He answer your prayer?

Let your puppets take it over from here.

Help them think of ways God has answered prayer. Remind them that God always answers in the way He knows best.

A Bible Verse to Learn

Don't be afraid; just believe. Mark 5:36

Talk to God

Thank God that He does answer your prayers, whether it's yes or no—or wait—or here's something better. If you don't understand why God seems to be saying no, or wait—tell Him about it. Be honest with Him. He really wants to know about all your feelings.

Can You Find This Story in the Bible?

Find Matthew 9:18-26; Mark 5:21-43; Luke 8:40-56.

The Man Who Couldn't See

Bartimaeus was blind, and there wasn't a chance in the world that he would ever see. He lived in Jericho, but he never saw the beautiful gardens and tall palm trees and busy market places. He sat by the side of the street and begged for money, but he never saw the crowds that went by or the people who stopped to give him a few coins. He lived in a world of BLACKNESS. And nobody seemed to care.

One day, Bartimaeus felt his way along the streets until he came to the big city gate. He sat down against the wall and began to beg. The people hurried by. He heard the clop-clop of the donkeys. Some sheep passed by so close he could touch their woolly sides. It was just like any other day. And then—

There was a sudden excitement in the air. Bartimaeus could FEEL it. People scrambled off to the side of the road. They backed up until they crowded against him. Everybody was talking at once.

"What is it?" cried Bartimaeus. "What's going on?" And he listened HARD to the voices around him.

"It's Jesus!"

"He's on His way to Jerusalem!"

"Out of the way, there. Back up!"

"There He is now!"

Oh, yes—Jesus. Bartimaeus could understand the excitement. No wonder! People followed Jesus everywhere. He taught them, and healed them—

He HEALED them—

Suddenly Bartimaeus' heart did a flip-flop. A great wild hope zoomed up inside of him. "Jesus—have mercy on me!" he shouted.

"Be quiet!" the people told him. "Stop shouting."

But Bartimaeus didn't stop. "Jesus—help me!" he cried, and he scrambled to his feet. And then—

Everyone grew quiet. Jesus had stopped, right in the middle of the road. He said something to His disciples. Bartimaeus could hear people mumbling. Then he could feel them jostling, moving sideways. He listened HARD. And then someone called, "Jesus wants to talk to you."

Bartimaeus could hardly believe it! He threw off his coat and he started to move forward. Then somebody took his arm. And the next thing he knew—

"What is it you want me to do for you?"

It was a voice that sent shivers of joy through Bartimaeus, right down to his toes.

It was JESUS!

"Lord, that I might receive my sight!" said Bartimaeus through the blackness. And then—Jesus spoke softly—

"Because you believe that I can do this for you, you shall see."

The blackness rolled away like a cloud. And there before Bartimaeus' eyes—stood Jesus! Bartimaeus could SEE Him. And all around him Bartimaeus could see—

men and women,
and bright-colored robes,
and the city gates—

oh, so many things, Bartimaeus didn't know where to look first! It was a great ocean of color! Then he looked back at Jesus. He said thank you to Jesus in every way he could think of. And when Jesus turned to walk down the road, Bartimaeus followed along with the crowd. He forgot how he had planned to spend the day. He forgot EVERYTHING—except that he loved Jesus—and he could SEE.

Bartimaeus had been blind. And there wasn't a chance in the world that he would ever see—until Jesus came along. Now he could see everything—like an ocean of color. But best of all—he could see JESUS.

Tracy and Mike Talk It Over

Mike: Well, God sure healed that blind man in a hurry.

Tracy: What if that happened today?

Do you think God makes blind people see today?

Mike: He does sometimes. My parents have told me about it.

Tracy: Yes, but lots of people He doesn't heal. He just doesn't, and nobody knows why. Dad knows a blind man who prayed and asked God to heal him and God didn't. He's still blind.

Mike: Why do you suppose God didn't heal the man? Was it because the man didn't have enough faith?

Tracy: No. Because some people God heals don't have any faith at all. Or they don't have very much anyway. I've heard about people like that and they were surprised that they were healed. They didn't even expect to be healed.

Mike: Do you suppose it was because they were not good enough?

Tracy: That can't be because some people who are very good don't get healed and some people who are very bad do get healed.

Mike: Then what's the reason?

Tracy: I don't know. I asked my mom about this and she just said, "Let God be God." Whatever that means.

Mike: Maybe it means that God does what He knows is best and He doesn't have to give us the reasons.

Tracy: Well, He sure does know all the rest of our lives and how we're going to spend them.

Mike: Sure! Maybe He knows that some people are better if they don't get healed. What do you think?

Let your puppets take it from here. They may have some very good ideas of their own.

A Bible Verse to Learn

"My thoughts are not your thoughts, neither are your ways my ways," *declares the Lord.* Isaiah 55:8

Talk to God

Why not talk to God about things you wonder about? Maybe you can tell Him that you don't understand everything He does. You can even argue with Him if you want to. He doesn't mind. All He wants you to do is—trust Him!

Can You Find This Story in the Bible?

Find Mark 10:46-52 and Luke 18:35-43.

The Most Extraordinary Lunch in the World

Back in the land where Jesus lived, an ordinary boy started off on an ordinary hike, on an ordinary day. He didn't know it, but it was going to be the most important day in his life! His mother gave him an ordinary lunch. Oh, it was a VERY ordinary lunch. Five barley loaves and two little dried fishes!

He whistled along the hills and up and down the paths. He whistled his way clear down to the shores of Lake Galilee.

Then he stopped.

There was a bigger crowd of people than he had ever seen before—more than five thousand people! They weren't standing. They seemed to be GOING someplace. And being filled with an ordinary amount of curiosity, he asked where they were going.

"See that boat?" they said.

Somewhere along the shore of the Sea of Galilee Jesus fed over five thousand people—with the little lunch a boy gave him. We are not sure of the exact spot, but many people think it was the large grassy area in the foreground overlooking the Sea of Galilee. (Photo © Stacey Martin)

251

Sure enough, there was a boat in the middle of the lake, going toward the other side.

"Jesus is in that boat. We're going to the other side of the lake so we can be there when He lands!"

Jesus!

The boy didn't stop a minute. He whistled his way right along with the crowd so he could be there, too.

When Jesus and His disciples landed on the other side of the lake, the crowd grew very quiet. Jesus began to tell them stories. The boy stopped whistling and got way up front so he wouldn't miss a thing.

He listened through the afternoon. He was still listening as the long shadows began to tuck the hills in bed.

Then one of the disciples said to Jesus, "Send these people home. It is time for them to get bread for themselves, for they have nothing to eat."

And Jesus said, "Where can we buy bread?"

"Why, Master," they told Him, "if we took a man's paycheck for a WHOLE MONTH and spent it ALL on bread, there wouldn't be enough. Send them home."

But Jesus said, "No, give them something to eat. How much bread do you have? Go and see."

The disciples started toward the crowd.

The boy watched as they got closer to him. Closer. Closer. Then—

"I have my lunch!" he shouted. Just like that!

He held it up—and before you could say "five barley loaves—" a disciple had led him right—up—to JESUS!

The boy's hands trembled so, he almost dropped his lunch. But he reached out and put it in Jesus' outstretched hands.

Then he went back and sat down on the grass. And he watched hard. Everybody else in the crowd watched hard, too.

Jesus bowed His head and thanked God for the lunch. Then He began to break the barley loaves and fishes into pieces. And then a wonderful thing began to happen. The more pieces Jesus broke off, the more pieces were left!

The disciples began to pass them out to the people. And when the disciples came back, there were MORE pieces. There were just pieces and pieces and PIECES.

Even after everyone was fed, there was enough left to fill—
twelve baskets!

The boy looked at what was left over from his ordinary lunch.
It was hard to believe. He had started out on an ordinary hike on
an ordinary day. It had started out just like any other day. But it
turned out to be the most important day of his life.

Nothing was very ORDINARY when Jesus was around!

Tracy and Mike Talk It Over

Mike: Boy! Just imagine what that kid did with just a little bit of lunch—I mean what Jesus did with it! The boy didn't know when he gave his little lunch—what was going to happen!

Tracy: Yes, but things like that don't happen today.

Mike: Sure they do. They just happen in different ways.

Tracy: How do you mean?

Mike: Well, I asked my mom about this and she said, you can plant one little seed and grow a whole lot of stuff. Why, you could plant an apple seed and get a whole apple tree! And it's the same way when you give money to God.

Tracy: But all we have is nickels and dimes. Did you ever give a dollar?

Mike: Sure. At Christmas and birthdays and times like that when I get a lot of money, I give more.

Tracy: Okay, so do I. But what good does my little bit do!?

Let your puppets take it from here.

You may have to jog them a bit if they are stumped. Suggest various church projects, missionaries, feeding the hungry and other ways our offerings to God are used. See how many ways they can come up with as to how God uses the gifts we give Him.

A Bible Verse to Learn

God loves a cheerful giver. 2 Corinthians 9:7

Talk to God

Thank God for all the big things He's doing all around the world with your nickels and dimes. Your little bit could turn out to be something very exciting. Thank God for letting you have a part in the great things He is doing.

Can You Find This Story in the Bible?

Find Matthew 14:13-21; Mark 6:32-34; Luke 9:10-17; John 6:1-14.

The Good Samaritan

Who is your neighbor? The people next door? People across the street? In the next apartment? Do you know one of the most wonderful stories ever told about neighbors was told by Jesus Himself?

Yes, sir. Jesus was teaching a crowd of people and the people were asking questions—when suddenly a lawyer stood up. Now, he wasn't the kind of a lawyer like we think of today. This lawyer was a lawyer who taught the Jewish law in the Temple.

The lawyer spread his feet and dug his sandals in the ground and put his hands on his hips and he was ready for a good argument. He said, "Teacher, what must a man do to have eternal life?"

Jesus knew the man was trying to trap Him. He looked at the man and said, "Well, you teach the law in the Temple, what does your law say?"

The lawyer said, "Our first law says you should love the Lord your God with all your heart and with all your soul and with all your strength and with all your mind and your neighbor as yourself."

"You have answered correctly," Jesus said. "Now go and do it."

The lawyer began to suspect that he had walked himself right

into a trap! He had to trick Jesus somehow. So he straightened up and said, "And who is my neighbor?"

Jesus didn't answer him directly. He just began to tell this story . . .

A man went down from Jerusalem to Jericho.

Oooooh. A low groan went through the crowd. The only direct road from Jerusalem to Jericho was about 20 miles, but it was one of the most dangerous roads in the entire country. In the first place, Jerusalem was way up high, thousands of feet above sea level. And Jericho was way down low, below sea level. The road went down so steeply that even a sure-footed donkey would skid his way all the way down. And the road had sharp hair-pin turns in it so you couldn't see what was ahead. It had enormous rocks on either side—a hiding place for ROBBERS.

The man wound his way down this very dangerous road. Sometimes he stopped, startled at a noise, and then he went on his lonely way. And then—

Wait a minute—wait a minute.

Suddenly the little ground creatures were running. The little lizards that had been on the rocks were scurrying away. Somebody was up there, somebody was—

The man stopped. He didn't know whether to go on or go back. And while he was still trying to make up his mind what to do, some robbers jumped at him and wrestled him to the ground!

OOF! They got his money belt. They even took off his clothes—RIP! They kicked him around the road to make sure he was dead. And then they clammered back up the rocks and were gone.

Silence, silence. The man lay there, as limp as a noodle—but there was no one to help him.

Then suddenly—what was that? It was the clop-clop of a donkey's hoofs coming down the road. Riding on the donkey was one of the priests of the Temple. He came around the bend and saw the man lying in the road—

Bits and parts of the ancient Roman road from Jerusalem to Jericho still remain today. The roads usually ran along the upper ridges of the valleys. People traveling down in the valleys were often attacked by robbers who jumped out from hiding places in the hills. (Photo © Stacey Martin)

The priest stopped his donkey for a minute—but only for a minute. *The man is probably dead,* he thought.

Now there was a law that said if a priest touched a dead body, he was considered "unclean" for seven days, and he could not serve in the Temple. And serving in the Temple was an important job. It meant a lot to the priests. It certainly meant a lot to THIS priest, because he passed by on the other side of the road and went on his way.

There was a silence again for a while. And then—

Someone else coming down the road. This time it was a Levite. Now a Levite served in the Temple, too, so he had the same problem the priest had. And he did the same thing the priest did.

Alas, it looked as if the poor, wounded man was going to lie there and die all alone because nobody cared for him.

But wait. The sound of a donkey's hoofs! Again!

This time the traveler was—a Samaritan! Now this fellow did not have to serve in the Temple, but he had a different problem. The Jews hated the Samaritans, and the Samaritans didn't like the Jews very much either. So there was no reason for this Samaritan to care about the poor, wounded Jew lying in the road. There was no reason for him to stop. But wait—

The Samaritan DID stop! He stopped without even thinking about it twice! And he ran over to the dying man. When the Samaritan saw that the man was still alive, he bound up his wounds as best he could, and he—HUP—flopped the man up on the donkey. And then very slowly and carefully he stumbled his way down around the curves until he finally came to an inn. He went inside the inn and said to the innkeeper, "Quick, quick, I've got to have some help."

And the innkeeper sent out some servants and everybody got busy at once. They huffed and they puffed and they lugged and they tugged and they finally got the poor dying man into the inn and put him to bed. They poured medicine in the rest of his wounds and bound them up. Then the Samaritan said to the innkeeper, "I'm going to stay here tonight and take care of him."

And do you know that good man, that Samaritan, sat by the dying man's bed and took care of him all night? And that wasn't all.

In the morning, he gave the innkeeper a handful of coins. "I'll be on my way now," he said. "You see that this man is taken care of until he is well. And if this isn't enough money, I'll pay you the rest when I come back this way again."

The story was finished. The crowd was silent, waiting. And Jesus looked, eyeball to eyeball, at the lawyer who had asked Him, "Who is my neighbor?"

Jesus said, "Which of the three men was the dying man's neighbor?"

Everybody looked at the lawyer. And the lawyer shifted his feet and stared at the ground. He was trapped. He finally had to say it.

"The one who showed mercy on him. The one who was kind."

"Again you have answered correctly," Jesus said. "Now you go and do the same."

Everyone looked at the lawyer and then back at Jesus again. For they had all learned a great lesson.

That's one of the most beautiful stories of what a neighbor is, that has ever been told. Who is your neighbor? The people next door? Across the street? In the next apartment?

No, your neighbor is anybody who is in trouble. Anybody who needs help.

Tracy and Mike Talk It Over

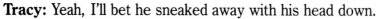

Mike: Boy, I'll bet that lawyer's face was red.

Tracy: Yeah, I'll bet he sneaked away with his head down.

Mike: But how does that fit us today? Nobody who lives anywhere near me needs help. You don't run into people every day who are lying on the road after being beaten up by robbers. So how does this story fit us today?

Tracy: I can't think of anything, except maybe we're helping people in ways we don't even know about. Can you think of anything?

Mike: No. Except that my mom and dad give blood to the Red Cross. Is that a way to be a neighbor to someone in trouble?

Tracy: Sure it is. And there are lots of other things we do through our church. Think, Mike, think!

Let your puppets take it from here.
Let them tell about people they know of who need help.

A Bible Verse to Learn

Love your neighbor as yourself. Luke 10:27

Talk to God

Talk to God about ways you can be kind to someone in need. Then ask God to help you think of some more people you can help. Tell Him what you have learned from this beautiful story and thank Him for showing you what a good neighbor really is.

Can You Find This Story in the Bible?

Find Luke 10:25-37.

An Exciting Day in Jerusalem

The disciples had no way of knowing what an exciting day this was going to be. It started out just like any other trip.

They left the little village where they had been staying, early in the morning. It was ordinary enough. Just Jesus and His disciples. As they walked along the road, people began to join them. The day was quiet and bright and blue. The disciples could hardly notice the excitement at first. They could just sort of FEEL it beginning.

It began when Jesus asked two of His disciples to go ahead to the next village and get a donkey. "Not just ANY donkey," He told them. "There's a CERTAIN donkey. Untie him and bring him to me."

The disciples went to the village—and it was exactly as Jesus had said. They brought the donkey back to Jesus—and that was when the excitement began to grow a little.

Some of the people took off their bright-colored robes and folded them across the donkey's back for Jesus to sit on. Now

Jesus looked like a KING, as they went down the road toward Jerusalem. More and more people began to follow along.

Old people.

Young people.

And CHILDREN.

And the excitement began to grow a little more.

Somebody took off his robe—and spread it on the ground in front of Jesus.

Then somebody else did.

And somebody else.

Then they began to cut branches from palm trees.

And wave them in the air.

And spread them on the road.

Until the road was covered with bright-colored robes and branches and branches and more branches.

Now a sight like that was too exciting for people to keep to themselves. The news spread ahead to Jerusalem. And when Jesus and His disciples got to the gates of Jerusalem—EVERYBODY was out to meet them! And the excitement grew and burst out—

like great swelling MUSIC.

The people were packed on both sides of the streets—the children in front so they could see. And they threw flowers.

And spread out leaves.

And waved palm branches.

And sang!

They sang, "Hosanna in the highest. Blessed is He who comes in the name of the Lord!"

And from the city gates to the great Temple with the golden roof—that song was in the air. The children sang it in the streets.

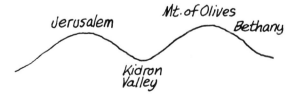

Jesus left the little village of Bethany to travel the path shown in the photo. It went up over the top of the Mount of Olives (in background) and down the other side to Jerusalem. Jerusalem is on a hill just across from the Mount of Olives. (Photo © Joyce Thimsen)

They sang it in the Temple courts.
They filled the air with it.
It was one of the most exciting days they'd ever had in Jerusalem.
The old people
 and young people
  and children
all wanted Jesus to know how much they loved Him!
 And they TOLD Him so!

Tracy and Mike Talk It Over

Mike: Wouldn't it have been fun to be there that day—to sing praises to Jesus?

Tracy: Yeah! And I would have sung the loudest of all!

Mike: Me, too! Wasn't it great that the children were included?

Tracy: Yeah! It makes me feel kind of special to know that Jesus likes to have children praise Him!

Mike: My mom says singing isn't the only way to praise Jesus. Can you think of any other ways to praise Him?

Tracy: Well, I can praise Jesus in Sunday School, that's easy.

Mike: Yeah, that's easy. But can you think of ways to praise Him during the week? I mean every day?

Tracy: Well, let's try. I bet I can think of more things than you can.

Mike: I'll bet you can't. Let's think of some things and see who comes up with the most.

Tracy: Let's start out with the morning, when you first get up.

Let your puppets take over and see who comes out ahead.

Some Bible Verses to Learn

It is good to praise the LORD. Psalm 92:1
Give thanks to the LORD for he is good. Psalm 107:1
Sing to the LORD with thanksgiving. Psalm 147:7

Talk to God

Tell God how much you love Him. Thank Him for everything He's done for you. And ask Him to remind you of some things you haven't thought of yet.

Can You Find This Story in the Bible?

Find Matthew 21:1-17; Mark 11:1-11; Luke 19:29-40; John 12:12-19.

The Saddest Day

O h, that was a glad day, when Jesus rode into Jerusalem on the donkey and people spread their robes and waved palm branches and the children sang and sang until the music seemed to rise to the very skies! It seemed absolutely impossible that anything dreadful could happen after such a glad day.

But it did.

It all began with some people who did not believe that Jesus is the Son of God. It would have been quite dreadful enough if they just didn't believe it, and let it go at that. But they didn't stop there. They sent a band of soldiers after Jesus. And the soldiers caught Him in a garden where He was praying to God. And they arrested Him and dragged Him before the ruler. And the ruler had Him tied to a post and whipped. It would have been dreadful enough if they had stopped THERE. But they did not.

When the ruler asked the people what they wanted to do with Jesus—

Some people cried out, "Kill Him!"

Then more people cried out, "Kill Him!"

Then MORE people cried out, "KILL HIM!"

They cried it out louder and louder and LOUDER.

Until there was such confusion and noise and shouting that it seemed to rise to the very skies, just the way the singing had done on that glad day!

But this was different from the singing. This was different from the glad day.

They made a big wooden cross. They dragged Jesus down into the street. They made Him carry the cross through the city. They took Him to the hill of Calvary just outside the city of Jerusalem. And there on that hill, they nailed Him to the cross by His hands and His feet. And they put the cross in a hole in the ground, so it stood up straight and tall. And there they left Him to die.

It seemed incredible!—hard to believe! Jesus was dead. JESUS was dead!

It was all over. All the gladness was over.

Jesus' friends took Him down from the cross. They carried Him—oh so tenderly—to a garden tomb—a little cave that was carved in the rocky hillside. And there they wrapped Him in soft clean cloths. And there they left Him.

The soldiers rolled a HUGE stone over the door of the tomb. And Jesus' friends went home.

Jesus was gone. And with Him, all the gladness was gone. Jesus' friends felt that there was no more gladness, anywhere in the world, anymore.

It was the saddest day in the world. But little did they know— there was a GLAD day coming! Just around the corner! The GLADDEST day in the world!

Tracy and Mike Talk It Over

Mike: Boy, that sure was the saddest day in all the world.

Tracy: It only SEEMED like the saddest day. God wasn't finished yet, remember?

Mike: Yeah, I remember. My mom and dad told me to THINK BACK why Jesus left His home in heaven and came to earth to die on the cross. He did this because He loves us so much.

Tracy: Sure. This is what it means when the Bible says that Jesus Christ came to be our Saviour.

Mike: So this all had to happen just the way God said it would. I suppose God knew what He was doing all right, but it's still very sad.

Tracy: No, it isn't really. It shows how much God loves us.

Let your puppets take over from here. You may have to explain if they still don't understand why Jesus died on the cross.

A Bible Verse to Learn

For God so loved the world [that means you] *that he gave his one and only Son, that whoever* [that means you again] *believes in him shall not perish but have eternal life.* John 3:16

Talk to God

Thank God for what He has done for you. Ask Him to help you understand His plan. Then thank Him that He loves you so much that He sent Jesus to die—for YOU.

Can You Find This Story in the Bible?

Find Mark 15:1-47; Luke 23:33-49; John 19:30.

The Gladdest Day

The day started out to be sad. It was still the saddest time in the world for Jesus' friends. Some of them were SO sad that they got up early in the morning and hurried back to the tomb in the garden where they had left Jesus' body—the tomb with the stone rolled in front of it. They knew it was all over and Jesus was dead. But they had spices and sweet perfumes for Him, and they hoped they'd find someone to roll the stone away.

When Jesus' friends hurried to the garden, all they expected to see was a tomb with a huge stone rolled over the doorway. But when they got there—

The great stone door of the tomb had been rolled away! And Jesus was GONE!

At first they just stood there, STUNNED.

And then they all did different things.

One of them turned on her heels and ran. Her name was Mary Magdalene. And she wasn't just running away. She was running to tell two other special friends.

The rest of them went into the tomb, and—

Surprise of all surprises!

There were two ANGELS inside!

Jesus' friends just stood there, absolutely speechless. They couldn't say a thing.

ANGELS!

And before Jesus' friends could find their voices, the angels said, "He is not dead. He is alive. He is RISEN—just as He told you He would be."

Well, Jesus' friends just stood there, stunned. And then THEY turned on THEIR heels and ran, just as Mary Magdalene had done.

Then the garden was quiet.

But not for long.

First, the two special friends Mary Magdalene had run to tell, came back. One of them stood and looked in the tomb. The other one went right inside. And sure enough. Everything Mary had told them was true. The cloth Jesus had been wrapped in was there, all neat and in order, and the cloth that had been wrapped around His head was folded neatly. But HE was gone. They went out of the garden, amazed.

Then the garden was quiet again.

But not for long.

For last of all, Mary Magdalene came back. And she stood there by the tomb crying. Then she looked inside and saw two angels.

"Why are you crying?" asked the angels.

And Mary said, "Because I do not know where Jesus is."

And then—

Suddenly she realized that there was somebody standing just behind her. She turned around. It was a man, but in the early morning half-darkness she did not know who it was. She thought perhaps He might be the gardener.

"Why are you crying?" He asked.

"And who are you looking for?"

This empty tomb (grave) is cut out of a hillside. Can you find the trough where a heavy stone was rolled in front of the doorway? We do not know for sure the location of the tomb where Jesus was buried. It may have been this tomb or it may have been one like it. But we do know for sure that Jesus is no longer in the tomb—He is alive! (Photo © Frances Blankenbaker)

"Oh," said Mary, "I'm looking for Jesus. Do YOU know where they have taken Him?"

And the stranger said softly—oh so softly and lovingly—"Mary." Just like that.

And the MINUTE He said her name—"Mary"—she knew who He was.

It was JESUS! He was alive! Oh, joy!

"Jesus!" said Mary. It couldn't be true. But it WAS. He was standing right there. He was looking at her. And He SPOKE to her again.

"Go tell my friends that I'm alive," He said, "and that I'm going to heaven—just as I said I would."

And she did!

Oh, it was a GLAD day after all! It was a GLAD day! It was the GLADDEST day in the world!

Do you know what?

It was the first EASTER SUNDAY!

Tracy and Mike Talk It Over

Mike: Wow! Jesus is alive!

Tracy: I know it. My mom told me this and my Sunday School teacher told me this and they got it right from the Bible. So it's true.

Mike: You bet; if it says so in the Bible, then it's true.

Tracy: Well then, since Jesus is alive, He can speak to us and He can still help us in our lives today.

Mike: Can you think of some ways He does that?

Let your puppets take it from there. You may have to jog them a bit to get them started. Jesus speaks to us in the Bible, in our thoughts, etc.

A Bible Verse to Learn

Jesus said, *"And surely I will be with you always, to the very end of the age."* Matthew 28:20

Talk to God

Thank God that Jesus is alive today and we can talk to Him and listen to Him and talk to each other about Him.

Can You Find This Story in the Bible?

Find Matthew 28:1-20; Mark 16:1-20; Luke 24:1,2; 13-53; John 20:10-18.

The Best News!

Yes, Easter was the gladdest day in the world. Jesus had come out of the tomb alive. Mary had seen Him. And she had run to tell all His friends, just as He had asked her to.

And after that His friends saw Him—not every day as they used to—but at the most surprising times!

One time two of them were just walking along the road on their way to a town called Emmaus—and there He was—walking along the road!

One time some of them just got back from fishing all night—and there He was—on the shore!

One time some of them were gathered together in a room in Jerusalem—and there He was—right in the room!

And then, ONE time—

They were with Him on the top of a mountain (the Mount of Olives)—when suddenly—

Jesus began to rise up into the air, right before their very eyes! Up—up—UP—until a big cloud covered Him up and He was GONE!

Jesus was standing on the Mount of Olives when He began to rise up into the air to go back to heaven. Can you picture Him rising—and then the cloud covering Him up? This photo shows how the Mount of Olives looks today. The church with the mosaic on the front and olive trees to the side of it (down near the road) are in the Garden of Gethsemane. (Photo © Gil Beers)

275

Why they just stood there staring at the sky.
 They were absolutely SPEECHLESS.
  And while they were staring—
   Two angels suddenly stood right alongside them!
    "Why are you staring up into heaven?" the two angels said.
     "Jesus is coming back again. Don't you remember?
      He's coming back again
      exactly the same way you just saw Him go—
      through the clouds!"

And then they DID remember.

Of course! Jesus had told them—a long, LONG time ago that He was going away. And they had been so sad.

"Going away?" they had said. "Going AWAY? Oh, NO!" And then they had all talked at once. "We will go with you," they had said.

And Jesus had looked at their sad faces, and oh, His eyes had been so KIND. "You cannot go with me NOW," He said. "But SOME day, you can."

"Ahhhhh—SOME day," they had thought. And then they had wanted to know—

Where was He going?

What was it LIKE?

And He had told them:

"I'm going to get a new home ready for you. It will be more beautiful than this world. More beautiful than anything you have ever SEEN. Or than anything you could ever IMAGINE." And He had gone on to tell them about heaven, where no one will ever be sick and no one will ever cry and no one will ever be unhappy. "And some day you can come and live there with me forever." He had said.

Of course!

They remembered, they remembered—

They couldn't be with Him NOW. But SOME DAY—

They remembered, they remembered—And they ran and ran to tell all the people!

Tracy and Mike Talk It Over

Mike: Just imagine. Jesus spoke to all those people after He rose from the dead and came out of the tomb.

Tracy: Yes! And some of them actually saw Him go up into heaven—right before their very eyes.

Mike: And He told them about heaven—but He said that it was even more wonderful than we can even imagine!

Tracy: But what happened to the people He left behind? What happened to His disciples?

Mike: I wondered about this, too, and I asked my dad. And he told me that after Jesus left, they weren't called disciples anymore. They were called APOSTLES.

Tracy: Whatever does THAT mean?

Mike: Well, an apostle means ONE WHO IS SENT FORTH.

Tracy: Then that must mean that they were supposed to go forth and tell all the people. How did you know about apostles? You're so smart.

Mike: No, I'm not that smart. My dad told me. And he told me that the whole rest of this book tells about the apostles and how they did that very thing. Boy, did they ever have exciting adventures!

Tracy: I can hardly wait. But while we're waiting, can you think of some ways that we can "go forth" and do the same thing?

Have your puppets take it from here.

Help them name some people they can tell the good news about Jesus.

A Bible Verse to Learn

Jesus said, *"I will come back and take you to be with me that you also may be where I am."* John 14:3

Talk to God

Thank God for His wonderful plan for Jesus to be born, to grow to be a man, to teach us about God, to die on the cross for us, to live again, to prepare a place for us in heaven—and to come back again! Then ask God to help you tell others this good news.

Can You Find This Story in the Bible?

Find Mark 16:19, 20; Luke 24:50-53; Acts 1:4-9.

The Gift that Was Better than Gold

Do you remember the story way back when Jesus was born? That was exciting news. Do you remember all the miracles Jesus did and the people He healed? He gave His followers the power to perform miracles and to heal people. Remember? And do you remember when He rose from the dead and was taken up to heaven?

Now all of this is so wonderful it's hard to imagine that anything more wonderful could happen. But it did.

It looked like an ordinary day in the city of Jerusalem. The washings were blowing in the sun on the rooftops, the shops were open on the little crooked streets, and outside the Temple in the courtyard, people were coming and going to pray and to worship God. And what a hustle and bustle it was!

The only one who was not bustling about was the beggar who sat at one of the big gates that led into the Temple. Friends carried him there every morning and sat him down to beg for money from the people who passed by. The poor man was a cripple. His feet and ankles were limp and useless, and they had been that way ever since he was born. He had never, never been able to walk, and

279

there wasn't a chance in the world that he ever would. He had no way of knowing, of course, that in just minutes something very wonderful was going to happen to him. He had no way of knowing that two men who were coming toward him were going to do something that would change his whole life.

For these two men were followers of Jesus. One of them was named Peter, and the other was named John. And wherever they went, excitement was sure to follow.

Yes, indeed.

When the lame man stretched his hands up toward Peter and John and begged for money, he expected them to walk right by without a glance, or maybe, just maybe, drop a coin into his hand, but he never expected what really happened. For Peter and John stopped in their tracks, and looked at him eyeball to eyeball. The Bible tells us that "Peter looked straight at him"— and that means he really STARED. The beggar looked back at Peter, trembling, and what happened next sent his head spinning.

"Silver and gold I do not have," said Peter, "but what I DO have, I give to you." And before the lame man could gather his senses, Peter went on. "In the name of Jesus Christ, WALK!"

Walk? WALK? That was enough to shake you out of your sandals. But what happened next was even more shocking. For Peter took the lame man by his right hand and pulled him to his feet and—

The lame man stood for a moment in amazement. Then he took a step. And then he began to WALK. His limp ankles that had been like wet noodles were now strong again. The man jumped up in the air. "I'm walking, I'm WALKING!" he cried.

And the people around him—

"What's going on?"

"It's that lame man, made to walk."

"It's the lame man who's been at the gate for years."

"He's ALWAYS been lame."

The crippled man was sitting outside the Temple gate called Beautiful (first gate in photo). This was the eastern gate between the Court of the Women (court just inside this gate) and the Court of the Gentiles (outer court). Gentiles (people who were not Jews) and Jews who did not meet certain requirements could not go any farther into the Temple than the Court of the Gentiles. They could not go through the Beautiful Gate. (Photo of model of Temple at Holyland Hotel, Jerusalem, Israel, by Joyce Thimsen.)

"Ever since he was born."

"He's walking, he's walking."

"He's JUMPING."

And then they stared at the lame man in astonishment. "What's happened to you?" But all the man could say was, "Praise God." It was all he could think of to say.

But that was quite enough at the moment. For he probably said it a thousand times more—for the rest of his life.

Tracy and Mike Talk It Over

Mike: Wow! Wasn't that SOMETHING?

One minute the man's ankles were like wet noodles—

Tracy: And the next minute he was WALKING!

Mike: Who do you think gave Peter and John all that power?

Tracy: My Sunday School teacher says it was God. When Jesus left the disciples He gave THEM the same power God had given HIM.

Mike: Yup. And He told them to go tell everybody about Him.

Tracy: And after that they were called apo—apo—apo—

Mike: Apostles. A—paaa—sils.

Tracy: A-PAAAA-sils. I got it.

Mike: Do you think people have the same power today?

Tracy: I think some people do. Sure they do. People get healed all the time.

Mike: ALL the time?

Tracy: Well some of the time. Every once in awhile.

Mike: Maybe God lets miracles happen once in awhile just to remind people that He has all power. When the people saw the lame man walking, they knew that only God could make the man well. My dad says that after the man was made well, hundreds of people listened to Peter tell about Jesus—and lots of them believed in Jesus.

Tracy: Yeah. That miracle sure helped a lot of people believe in Jesus.

Mike: Can you think of any miracles that you've seen? Or maybe heard about?

Let your puppets take it from here.

Let them talk about things God has done that no one else could do—and how seeing God's power helps people believe in Him.

A Bible Verse to Learn

You are great and do marvelous deeds; you alone are God.
Psalm 86:10

Talk to God

Praise God for His wonderful power. Thank Him for using His power to help us learn about Him and about His Son, Jesus. Tell God how much you love Him.

Can You Find This Story in the Bible?

Find Acts 3:1-26; 4:1-4.

The People Who Prayed and PRAYED

Rhoda, did you put enough oil in the lamps?"

"Yes, my mistress," Rhoda said. She had filled the lamps with oil, and swept the floors, so that everything would be ready for the people who were going to gather there that night.

These were very important people; they were followers of Jesus. And Rhoda? Well, she was only a little servant girl. She didn't feel she was important at all. She knew what was going on all right—she kept her eyes and ears open. She knew just about everything that was going on.

What was going on right now was important. In fact, it was earthshaking. For Peter, one of Jesus' followers, was locked up in prison. Not because he had done anything wrong; no—the wicked ruler of the city had locked him up just because he was a follower of Jesus. Peter was locked up in prison just for the night, and that sounds good—except for one thing: the ruler had ordered that Peter be killed in the morning!

Rhoda knew all this as she let each visitor in. The followers of Jesus kept coming and coming and coming—until the room was crowded with them. They sat all over on couches and mats and pillows—and all over the floor—until there was hardly room for

them to move. But as best they could, they got on their knees, and they cried out to God to save poor Peter.

They prayed all evening. They prayed
    and prayed
      and PRAYED!

On and on, the minutes went by and the hours went by.

And Rhoda was allowed to stay up and pray right along with them.

They knew that if Peter was let out of prison, he would come straight there to the house to let them know about it. But he didn't come.

And he didn't come—
And he didn't come—

We'll find out what happens in the next story.

Tracy and Mike Talk It Over

Tracy: Boy, that story sure leaves Peter in a tight spot.

Mike: It leaves those poor people in a tight spot, too. They've been praying for hours and hours, and Peter hasn't come. Do you think he will?

Tracy: Well, there's something going on. That's for sure, but they don't know yet what it is.

Mike: Do you suppose that when we ask God to do something for us and He makes us wait and wait, that there is something going on that we don't know anything about?

Let your puppets take it from here.

If children cannot think of anything specific in their own lives, you might tell of an incident where people have prayed for missionaries and found out much later that the missionaries were saved from danger. One example is a missionary pilot who couldn't find his way through the clouds to land his plane. Suddenly, the clouds parted and he could see where to land. Some time later, the missionary received a letter from a lady who said she woke up one night and felt she should pray for him. She did pray, and she wondered what was happening in his life at that particular time. When the missionary read the day and hour the woman gave, he knew it was exactly the time he was trying to find his way through the clouds to land! He told the lady how God answered her prayer.

A Bible Verse to Learn

I will call to you, for you will answer me. Psalm 86:7

Talk to God

Thank God that you can pray, and ask Him to protect other people. Thank Him for any time you can think of where He has done this. Ask Him to give you the patience to wait if He does not answer right away. Thank Him for the times when you might be in danger—and other people are praying for you.

Can You Find This Story in the Bible?

Find Acts 12:1-4, 12.

The Mysterious Way God Answered

Peter sat inside his prison cell, his chin on his chest, staring at a cricket that was scurrying across the floor. He watched it until it got to the door and then disappeared under the crack. The cricket was free. Peter was not. For when morning came, he would be killed. King Herod himself had ordered it.

Peter changed his position painfully. Every muscle in his big body ached. He was chained to soldiers, one on each side. He slid down, his chains rattling until he was lying almost flat. In a few minutes, he was asleep.

He knew that back in the big house, across town, his friends were praying for him. And indeed they were.

And while they prayed, Peter slept. And even while he was sleeping, he thought of Jesus. He remembered all the wonderful things that Jesus had done.

And he thought of his friends back there in the house. They'd still be praying, no matter how late it got. They would still be . . .

Peter felt a sharp slap on his side. His eyes flew open. There was a bright light in his cell. A man was standing over him.

Why—why—it was an ANGEL!

"Quickly," the angel said, "get up! Put on your shoes."

Peter started to grope for his sandals. He did it slowly so he wouldn't pull on his chains and wake his guards. But what was this? His chains had fallen away from his wrists and were lying on the floor. His hands were free.

"Now, quickly, Peter, put on your coat, and follow me." The angel's orders were sharp; he meant business. Peter was jolted into action. He grabbed his coat. And he scrambled up. And he bolted after the angel. But he was still in a daze.

They went through the first cellblock—

And the second—

And got to the iron gate that led to the street. Peter waited for the angel to open it, but he did not. Instead, the gate opened all by itself!

Peter went through with the angel. He could not quite believe what was happening. Any minute, he thought, he'd wake up. The angel walked on, and Peter walked beside him in silence.

Finally, he turned to speak to the angel—

But the angel was gone!

And Peter was alone. He stood stockstill for a moment, trembling. Then as soon as he could make his legs behave, he hurried up the dark street and headed for the house where he knew his friends were praying. He walked until he saw the light in the windows. Then he hurried even faster, until he got to the courtyard gate. He listened for a minute to make sure no one was following him. Then he knocked, very softly at first, then he knocked louder. And he waited.

And waited— And waited—

And we'll find out what happened in the next story!

Tracy and Mike Talk It Over

Tracy: Wow! So that was the other side of the story.
Mike: That was the part that the people didn't know about.
Tracy: And Peter was flabbergasted.
Mike: Well, you would be flabbergasted, too, if anything like that ever happened to you. Can you think of anything that has happened to you when God saved you from danger and you were flabbergasted?

Let your puppets take it from here. (Parent/teacher: If children cannot think of anything in their own lives, be prepared with an incident about people you know who have been rescued from danger.)

A Bible Verse to Learn

He will call upon me and I will answer him; I will be with him in trouble, I will deliver him. Psalm 91:15

Talk to God

Thank God that He is still in the business of rescuing people and answering prayer. Ask Him to send His angels to help people you know who might be in danger. Thank Him for caring for us.

Can You Find This Story in the Bible?

Find Acts 12:5-13.

A Surprise
for Rhoda

R hoda raised her head for a minute and yawned a long silent
yawn. Soooooo sleepy. She squirmed around to a sitting
position to help wake herself up. She bent her knees up and rested
her elbows on them. She bunched her closed fists into her cheeks
and pressed hard. Then she yawned again. This seemed like the
longest night she had ever known. She did not want to sleep, but
she had a feeling that any minute she was going to drift off. And
then she thought of her friend Peter, in a prison cell, chained to
two soldiers, and when morning came, he would be killed. That
jolted her awake. But after a few minutes she found herself drifting
off again. And then—

Wait a minute! What was that?

Someone knocking. Someone knocking at the outside courtyard
gate.

"Someone's knocking at the outer gate," she cried, and
everyone in the room snapped to attention.

She was nearest the door. She got up quickly and headed for
the door, stepping over people as she went. Outside in the
courtyard, she headed for the gate. Sure enough, someone had
been knocking all right—someone was still knocking.

"Who is it, please?" she called out, but softly. Softly, hardly daring to breathe—

"It's Peter!"

"WHAAAT? Peter? Could it be?" It was!

"It's Peter," he said again. "Open the gate."

Rhoda stood there for a moment, stunned. Then instead of opening the gate—

She ran back inside the house.

Inside the house she leaned against the door, gasping. "It's Peter!" she blurted out at last.

"No!" they cried. "It can't be!"

"But it is," she insisted. "I heard his voice with my own ear drums!"

"You're out of your mind, Rhoda. You must have seen his angel," they said. But then—knock, knock, KNOCK!

Someone was still out there!

Jesus' friends got stuck in the doorway trying to go out and see. They rushed across the courtyard, stumbling over each other, crying and shouting—

And then they opened the outside gate. Sure enough, it was Peter, the sweat pouring down his face and into his beard.

"Peter! We've been praying for you all night."

"We thought it was your angel."

"Peter, oh, Peter!"

Their joy was wonderful, but their shouting was dangerous. Peter slipped inside the gate and closed it behind him. Then he raised his hands for them to shush.

"An angel let me out," he said softly.

Little Rhoda's hands went up to her mouth and her eyes opened so wide they seemed to be all white.

"Your eyes look like hardboiled eggs, Rhoda," Peter said, and he looked at her lovingly. "Isn't Jesus wonderful?"

Rhoda began to cry. She was overcome with love, and bleary with waiting.

Peter hugged her quickly and then began to talk in whispers to the other people. He explained that he had to go into hiding until the hubbub died down. Then he backed out of the gate and disappeared into the darkness.

Rhoda cried all the way back into the house. But her tears were tears of joy. For God had set Peter free and saved him from death! Surely, this was one of the most wonderful nights that Rhoda, the little servant girl, had ever known!

Tracy and Mike Talk It Over

Mike: Boy, oh, boy! What a night!

Tracy: It was sad. And funny, too.

Mike: How can a story be sad and funny at the same time?

Tracy: Well they prayed all night. And then when God answered their prayer, they didn't believe it. That was funny, I think.

Mike: Oh, I see. But it was sorta sad, too, because they didn't believe God.

Tracy: Have you ever had God answer a prayer for you—and it was so wonderful you couldn't believe it?

Mike: Well, after the prayer was answered, maybe I wouldn't want to ADMIT I didn't believe it.

Tracy: Well, think of some time when that happened to you. And admit that you didn't believe it.

Mike: I'll think of something. Give me a minute.

Have your puppets take it from here. (Parent/teacher: You might suggest an incident that happened to you.)

A Bible Verse to Learn

I will give you thanks, for you answered me. Psalm 118:21

Talk to God

Thank God that He still answers prayers for you—even today. Then thank Him for some special answer to prayer. Don't forget to thank Him for caring for you every day, whether or not you are in trouble.

Can You Find This Story in the Bible?

Find Acts 12:12-17.

There's Bad News in Damascus

When the bad news came, it hit Ananias and his friends like a thunderclap. They lived in the city of Damascus and they were followers of Jesus. And they met to talk about Him and learn about Him, and sing and pray to Him—and nobody bothered them very much. They felt quite safe. And then—

WHAM!

They heard the bad news.

It was about a man back in Jerusalem who absolutely HATED the followers of Jesus. His name was Paul,* and if he had been an ordinary man it would not have mattered so much. But he was a POWERFUL man with a great deal of AUTHORITY. If he wanted to, he could do a great deal of harm. And that's where the problem came in.

He WANTED to.

And the news that got back to Damascus was not good. This Paul person was acting like a crazy man. He was searching the houses in Jerusalem—up one street and down another—door to door—and having his men drag out anyone who was a follower of

---

*When we first read about this man, his name is Saul, but we will use the name everyone remembers him by—Paul.

Jesus. And he had them put in chains and thrown into prison. And NOW the news was that he had gone to the highest authorities, gotten official permission to travel to Damascus—and do the same thing to believers there!

This was terrifying.

The believers in Damascus didn't get the news the way we do on television. They got it through merchants and travelers who came by on camels and donkeys and in caravans. So they got the news in bits and pieces.

This dreadful man Paul was getting ready to make good his threats.

He had actually left Jerusalem with his men.

He was coming, he was coming, he was COMING—

He would be here any day now, any day—

It was enough to scare you right out of your sandals.

The believers knew they might be thrown into prison or maybe even killed.

But there was something they did not know. It was something unbelievable.

Wait until you hear about it in the next story.

Tracy and Mike Talk It Over

Mike: Were these people ever in trouble!

Tracy: All they know is that there's some powerful man who has the authority to kill people who love Jesus.

Mike: I'll bet something's going to happen to him while he's on his way. What do you think?

Tracy: Maybe he'll be killed or something. What do you think?

Mike: I don't know. But do you want to know what I think? I think that what they're worrying about isn't going to happen.

Tracy: Did you ever worry about something—and then when the time came, it didn't happen? What did you do? How did you feel?

Mike: Well, after I found out it didn't happen, I felt great, but BEFORE it didn't happen—I guess I just worried.

Tracy: What are some things you worry about?

Mike: I worry about earthquakes and floods and robbers—all sorts of things.

Tracy: I worry about things, too.

Mike: Do they ever happen?

Tracy: No, they don't happen, but I still worry that maybe they will happen.

Mike: Well, let's spill our worries. I'll spill mine if you'll spill yours. And let's be honest about it. I'll be honest if you'll be honest.

Let your puppets take it from here. (Parent/teacher: encourage your children to "spill out their worries." Children worry about rejection, about not being able to please a parent or a teacher, a new baby who is getting all the attention. Reassure your children and encourage them. This could be a revealing and rewarding session!)

Some Bible Verses to Learn

Do not be anxious about anything, . . . present your requests to God. Philippians 4:6
Cast all your anxiety on him because he cares for you.
1 Peter 5:7

Talk to God

Spill your worries out to God—your big ones and your little ones. Thank Him that He cares about all your worries—your big ones and your little ones. And thank Him that He loves you and cares about you.

Can You Find This Story in the Bible?

Find Acts 9:1,2,13,14.

The Strangest Thing Happened on the Way to Damascus

Paul was within sight of Damascus when it happened.

Suddenly—a great light!

A light more powerful and more brilliant than any light he had ever seen.

His horse stopped so suddenly that Paul slid down right over his neck and hit the ground like a sack of potatoes. The officers around him stopped, too. What was it?

Thunder?

They did not know.

A voice? Yes, it was a voice, but Paul was the only one who understood what it said. It was a voice—calling him by name. "Paul," it said—

Paul waited, trembling.

"Paul," the voice said again, "why are you fighting against me like this?"

Paul swallowed hard. "Who are you?" he said at last, and it came out like a croak.

"I am the One you've been fighting against. I am JESUS!!"

Paul just lay there in the dust, trembling.

"Now get up," the voice said.

Paul staggered to his feet.

"But, Lord," he began.

"Don't 'but' me," the Lord said, "and don't try to second guess me. Just do what you are told. I've had a hard enough time with you already.

"Now, here's what I want you to do."

Paul just listened, silent and shaken.

Then the light disappeared and the voice was gone.

"What was it?" Paul's officials asked. "It sounded like thunder."

"It was Jesus," Paul said. "He's for real, He really is the Son of God. He is REALLY for REAL."

And the way he said it—they knew that it was true.

Paul was on his way to Damascus when Jesus spoke to him. The photo shows one of the roads leading to Damascus. The snow-capped mountain in the background is Mount Hermon. (Photo © Stacey Martin)

"Take me into Damascus," Paul went on. "The Lord will show us where to go. But you'll have to lead me."

They stared at him in amazement. His eyes did not seem to be looking back at them at all. They seemed to be staring into space.

Good grief!

HE WAS BLIND!!!

Tracy and Mike Talk It Over

Mike: Wowwowwowwow!

Tracy: So the guy who was on his way to kill the people who loved Jesus—got stopped in his tracks! The Lord sure used a strange way to get his attention!

Mike: The Lord clobbered him!

Tracy: How do you suppose the Lord gets our attention today when He wants to tell us something?

Mike: When we read the Bible?

Tracy: Sure, and maybe when we're praying even.

Mike: Or maybe when we're just thinking about Him?

Tracy: Sure. Sometimes I think about somebody I don't like and then God reminds me of something NICE about that person that I SHOULD like. Sometimes that's how it happens. Can you think of some other ways?

Let your puppets take it from here.

Encourage them to think of some time when they disliked something or someone and got turned around in their thinking.

A Bible Verse to Learn

Love each other as I have loved you. John 15:12

Talk to God

Thank God that He speaks to you when you read the Bible and when you pray and when you think about Him. Think of some special time when He has done this for you.

Can You Find This Story in the Bible?

Find Acts 9:1-8.

A Special Message for Paul

Ananias lay sleeping, feeling as safe and snug as a mouse in a house where no cat lives—when suddenly—HE heard God's voice, too.

"Ananias—Ananias—"

"Yes, Lord," Ananias said, and got up on one elbow. He knew right away that it was the Lord speaking to him.

"Ananias," the Lord said, "wake up. There's something I want you to do."

"Yes, Lord, what is it? Anything. Just ask me."

"Get up and go over to the Straight street."

"Yes, Lord, got it."

"Go to the house of the man called Judas—"

"Yes, Lord, I know about him. He takes in people for lodging."

"Well, I want you to go there and ask for a man named Paul."

"Whaaaat?

"My Lord," Ananias sputtered, "that man is here in Damascus to have us all dragged back to Jerusalem and get thrown in jail— maybe even killed!"

"Not anymore," the Lord said. "I've had a little talk with him, and he is a changed man. He's also blind."

"Blind?! That must have been quite a talk."

"I've already told him," the Lord said, "that you were going to go there and pray for him to get his sight back."

And Ananias did not stop to argue. He shimmied into his outer clothing and laced up his sandals and walked swiftly through the streets until he got to the street called Straight. He knocked on the door of Judas' house. When it opened he expected an argument from Paul's officials, but they let him in without a word and led him to the room where Paul was. Ananias knelt down by the mat where Paul was lying, and put his hand on Paul's head. "Brother Paul," he said, "Jesus sent me here so that you would be filled with the very Spirit of God Himself. And so that you may get your sight back."

And right then and there—

In that split second—

Paul could see!

Paul didn't know what was going to happen when he started out on that journey. Ananias didn't know what was going to happen when he learned that Paul was on his way to Damascus. God DID know. He planned the whole thing. And He was watching over both of them every minute!

Tracy and Mike Talk It Over

Mike: Just look how that all came out. Can you imagine? It was like the whole story was tied up in knots—and God came along and untied every one.

302

Tracy: He sure did. Ananias and his friends didn't know what was going to happen.

Mike: No—all they knew was that some powerful guy was going to come to Damascus and kill them all off. And Paul didn't know what was going to happen to HIM while he was on his way, either.

Tracy: But then God jumped in and untied all the knots and straightened everything all out.

Mike: Didn't it all turn out just great?

Tracy: Yes, but nothing like that ever happens to us today.

Mike: But don't some things sometimes happen in our lives when everything seems to be all full of knots, and then God jumps in and unties them all? Think a minute. Think about some things that are all in knots and then God straightens them all out.

Tracy: Maybe I can think of something, but they don't seem important now.

Mike: Sure. They don't seem important after they're all straightened out and God has untied all the knots. Think about the knots.

Tracy: I'll try. Give me a minute.

Turn your puppets loose on this.

(Parent/teacher: You may have to prompt the children a bit. Share with them times in your own life when God straightened out difficult situations. Then encourage your children to talk about any difficult situations they may be facing.)

A Bible Verse to Learn

Great is our Lord and mighty in power. Psalm 147:5

Talk to God

Thank God for "knots" in your life. They may seem like little things to you, but they are are all very important to God and He wants to help. Thank Him for helping. And if you have any knots in your life that haven't been untied yet, tell Him about it. He cares!

Can You Find This Story in the Bible?

Find Acts 9:10-19.

Paul and Silas in Prison

It was dark inside the prison—thick walls, no windows, just huge heavy double doors in front. The two prisoners had been dragged there by soldiers— and dragged is a good word for it, for they had been beaten so badly they could scarcely stand. "These men are teaching things that are against our Roman law," the soldiers told the jailer as he unbolted the outer doors. "They're telling all the people about Jesus."

These men? These men? Who WERE these men? One of them was Paul. The other one was his companion, Silas.

"I'll keep them safe, all right," the jailer muttered. Then Paul and Silas were hauled into the inner prison.

They were chained to the walls by their hands. And their feet were locked into wooden frames. The jailer and the soldiers bolted the door and their footsteps faded away.

And Paul and Silas were alone in the blackness.

They couldn't say much at first. They hurt all over.

After a while, they lifted their faces and looked up into the darkness and they began to—

What do you think? Began to groan? Whine? Howl? No—they began to SING songs of PRAISE! Songs of praise to God!

The prisoners in the outer prison stopped their swearing and their groaning. What kind of men were THESE?

In the blackness of the inner prison—they were singing!

Were they crazy?

Singing and praising God!

Singing and—

Wait a minute. W-A-A-A-I-T a minute.

WHAT WAS THAT?!

Thunder? No, worse than thunder. The ground was ROCKING. The very walls of the prison were swaying back and forth.

Paul and Silas clutched at each other for support. Suddenly their feet went up in the air! Their feet were loose—and their hands, too! Their chains were broken. The wooden frames that held their feet were wrenched open. The cell door was torn from its hinges and sagged outward and crashed to the ground. An earthquaaaake!!!

And sure enough, it was.

And as Paul and Silas staggered to their feet and went out to the outer prison, they realized that the outer door had been torn loose, too. By this time the jailer had run down from his house that was alongside the prison, the ground still shaking beneath him. When he saw that the prison doors had been torn off, he stopped and stared, with his mouth open. That could mean only one thing: his prisoners had escaped. That meant he would have to pay with his life.

Then everything seemed to happen at once. A voice shouted at him from inside the prison: "Don't hurt yourself; we are all here." At the same moment his assistants came running with lighted torches. He grabbed one and peered inside. Sure enough, the prisoners were all there. And who should be standing in the midst of them but Paul and Silas, the men who had been arrested for talking about Jesus.

The poor jailer was terrified. He dropped his short sword and fell to his knees. "Tell me," he cried, "what must I do to be saved?" The answer was quick and sure. "Believe in the Lord Jesus Christ, and you'll be saved—and your whole family."

Incredible!

And what a joyful scramble followed. The jailer took Paul and Silas to his house. He bathed and bandaged their wounds. The jailer and his family were baptized. They fixed a meal for Paul and Silas to eat. Then they all talked and talked and TALKED about Jesus. The whole family was filled with joy because they believed in Jesus. The night of gloom had been turned into a night of rejoicing.

Tracy and Mike Talk It Over

Mike: What if you were locked in a prison that was like a dungeon?—locked in for something you didn't do? Do you think you could sing?

Tracy: I'm not so sure I could. No—I'm sure I couldn't. Could YOU sing?

Mike: Maybe they sang because they were sure they were going to get out?

Tracy: But they WEREN'T sure they were going to get out. They just went ahead and sang anyway.

Mike: Well, suppose you were in trouble and you weren't sure you were going to get out of it. All right, maybe you wouldn't SING. But could you trust God?

Tracy: I don't know. I don't know. I hope I would have enough sense to trust Him anyway. What do YOU think?

Have your puppets take it from here. And tell them to be absolutely honest.

A Bible Verse to Learn

I trust in God's unfailing love. Psalm 52:8

Talk to God

Talk to God about how you feel when you are in trouble. Be absolutely honest with Him. Tell Him about times when you can absolutely trust Him no matter what happens—and admit to Him where your feelings might be a bit shaky. He understands your feelings. Ask Him to help you. Be honest with yourself. And ask Him to give you more faith.

Can You Find This Story in the Bible?

Find Acts 16:22-34.

The Adventure that Couldn't Be Told

This is all about an ordinary boy who had a most EXTRAORDINARY adventure. He even got to be in the Bible because of it, though the Bible does not tell us his name. So we'll give him a name—we'll call him Jonathan.

Jonathan's story began when he saw the great apostle Paul being dragged off to prison. What? Again? Yes, indeed. Locked up in prison right there in Jerusalem.

When Jonathan saw this, he stopped, frozen in his tracks, for the great apostle Paul WAS HIS UNCLE!

Now it's quite possible that Jonathan and his family and friends prayed and asked God to send an angel or an earthquake or SOMETHING to get Paul out of prison. We don't know. But anyhow, nothing happened.

In fact, things began to get worse. For what Jonathan overheard in the Temple court the next day made him realize that if Uncle Paul's life was to be saved, God was going to have to use him—Jonathan—to do it. He had to somehow get into that prison and warn Uncle Paul.

It wasn't easy. Jonathan was scared to death. And when the guards led him to Uncle Paul's cell, he could hardly find his voice. Uncle Paul stretched his arms through the bars and took Jonathan by the shoulders.

"Uncle Paul," Jonathan whispered, "I've just heard something. They are planning to kill you."

"What do you mean?"

"I was just in the Temple and I overheard them. Some men have sworn not to eat or drink until you are dead. They are going to ask the court to send for you again and when you are on your way there, they will lie in wait for you there and jump the guards and KILL you before you ever get to the council—you'll be murdered!" It all came out in one breath.

"You're a brave lad to come here and tell me, Jonathan." Uncle Paul whispered.

"But you see, the Lord Himself came to me last night. He promised me that I would go to Rome to tell people there about Jesus. Now, Jonathan, if the Lord said I was going to Rome, I've got to live to get there, don't I?"

"Of, course, Uncle Paul!"

"Guard!" Paul cried out, "take this lad to the chief captain. He has something of great importance to tell him."

And then he turned to Jonathan. "Go with the guard and tell the captain everything you've told me, and *don't be afraid.*"

The next thing he knew, Jonathan was facing the chief captain

and his knees were like wet noodles. But he told the captain everything he had overheard.

And the captain believed him! He ordered soldiers! And horsemen! and spearmen! And he barked out his orders.

"You are to take the prisoner to Caesarea. Be ready to go tonight."

And that's exactly what they did.

That very night they sneaked Uncle Paul out of prison and carried him off to Caesarea, away from harm.

But alas!

The captain told Jonathan never to tell ANYBODY about what they had done.

And Jonathan promised he would not. Such a disappointment! But down in his heart he knew that God had rescued Uncle Paul from prison.

Not by an angel.

And not by an earthquake.

But by him, himself—JONATHAN!

Tracy and Mike Talk It Over

Mike: Boy, I LIKE this story. I like this story. Just think! It took a kid to straighten this mess all out!

Tracy: Well, it was God who straightened this mess all out. He just used a kid to do it.

Mike: I know. But just think—Jonathan was brave enough to do it.

Tracy: Still it was God who used a kid to do it.

Mike: We're just kids. Do you suppose God would ever use us to straighten out some mess?

Tracy: Well, God has never used me to straighten out some mess.

Mike: But suppose you had a friend who was headed for trouble. And you knew something nobody else did. And if you spoke up and told what you knew—maybe this guy wouldn't get in trouble. What would you do?

Paul was secretly taken to Caesarea, a seaport city that had been built by Herod the Great. This important city had kings' palaces, public buildings, a great amphitheater and a busy seaport. (Photo © Frances Blankenbaker)

311

Tracy: Well I suppose I would go to whomever I would have to go to and tell them all the truth—you're getting me all mixed up.

Mike: Why?

Tracy: Because I'm not sure I'd be brave enough to do it. Maybe it would wind up getting me into trouble. How do I know?

Mike: Would you be brave enough to do it even if it did get you into trouble?

Tracy: I don't know. Maybe I should tell somebody else about it and let HIM get in trouble. You've got me all mixed up. What would YOU do?

Turn your puppets loose on this. They may be stumped. They may have some very good ideas.

(Parent/teacher: Children are wiser than you think. Help them if you can. This one is a stickler!)

A Bible Verse to Learn

Be strong and courageous . . . , for the Lord your God will be with you. Joshua 1:9

Talk to God

Talk this over with God. Tell Him if you would be brave enough to tell the truth to get somebody out of a mess. Or tell Him if you would be scared. Be honest with Him. God doesn't care if you're brave or scared. But He cares very much if you are honest. And if you are scared, ask God to help you to be brave. Thank Him that He understands just exactly how you feel.

Can You Find This Story in the Bible?

Find Acts 23:11-35.

A Dangerous Journey

Well, God had kept His promise. And the apostle Paul was on a ship bound for Rome at last.

A nice soft breeze filled the sails, and the ship slid through the blue water, as if she were floating on clouds. Nothing could stop Paul now. Nothing could—

What was this?

It came without warning. The wind came swooping down from the north like a huge giant. The ship leapt through the waters like a frightened animal being chased and not knowing where to go. The wind lifted the ship up, up—to the top of huge giant waves—and then hurled her down again, down, down, down. And everyone gave up hope.

Everyone but Paul.

"Cheer up," he said, "for the Lord stood by my side last night and told me that everyone on this ship is going to be saved. Not one of you is going to die."

Well, they thought he must be crazy, but they didn't have to wait long to find out.

For that very night—

Listen! Was it—it couldn't be—but it was! The distant sound of water booming against land!

"Land!" they shouted, "Land"

When daylight finally came, they realized that there was land all right. They could see a sandy beach. But dead ahead were rocks—jagged rocks—killers, waiting to rip the ship apart.

Well, sir, you never saw sailors work so hard in your life. They were like a colony of ants, scampering about, following the captain's orders.

"Cut the anchor cables!"

"Untie the rudders!"

"Hoist the foresail!"

And the sailors did everything that sailors know how to do. And swung that ship around and it missed the rocks. It missed the rocks.

It missed the rocks!

But it hit a sandbar and RAN AGROUND!

Alas!

The ship was stuck fast in the sand and the rear end was in the water. Fierce crosscurrents grabbed hold of the tail end of the ship and ripped it apart as if it was made of paper!

There was a great C-R-E-A-K as the timbers tore loose. Then there was an ear-splitting noise of scraping, crunching, ripping, twisting—the ship was coming apart.

SHE WAS COMING APART!

Then there was an incredible tangle of men and splintering timber. And soldiers, sailors, passengers, prisoners, all jumped. Or slid. Or crawled. Or fell. Until one way or another, they were all pitched into the raging sea.

They went under the water. And came back up again. And went down under again. And came bobbing up again. Until finally, one by one, they were all tossed up on the sandy beach.

And there they lay, still, like a bunch of toy soldiers. Every one of them. Not a man had been lost.

Yes—it took a while—but Paul finally did get to Rome. He was a prisoner, but he was allowed to stay in his own rented house. He had soldiers with him. And wherever he went, he told everyone about Jesus. He told them, and told them and told them. And the Bible tells us that no one tried to stop him!

Tracy and Mike Talk It Over

Mike: Boy, that's the most exciting story about a shipwreck I ever read.

Tracy: I asked my dad about this and he says that it's the most exciting story about a shipwreck that has ever been written. Anywhere! But do you know what I like best? Paul never QUIT!

Mike: That's right! He never did! He wasn't afraid of ANYTHING!

Tracy: Sometimes I get scared.

Mike: But we shouldn't get scared, Tracy. God cares just as much about US as He did about PAUL.

Tracy: That's right! Let's think of some things we might be scared of. And ask God to help us to be brave and never to quit.

Let your puppets take it from here.

A Bible Verse to Learn

He cares for those who trust in him. Nahum 1:7

Talk to God

Thank God for caring for you in times of trouble. Ask HIM to help you never to be afraid and NEVER to QUIT.

Can You Find This Story in the Bible?

Find Acts 27:27-44; 28:30,31.

A STORY ABOUT JOHN—AND ABOUT YOU!

The Best News of All!

Adventures, ADVENTURES! The apostles had more adventures than we could fit into this book. Each one was exciting—but the very last one is the most exciting of all!

It happened to the apostle John while he was on the island of Patmos.* John was sent there as a punishment for talking too much about Jesus. John did not know it but he was about to become a part of the most exciting book in the whole Bible.

And this is how it happened.

John was all by himself. He was worshiping God. When suddenly, right behind him, he heard a voice. He turned around. And when he saw who it was—

He fell down FLAT.

It was JESUS!!!

---

*Patmos was an island that was used as a sort of prison by the Romans.

"Don't be afraid," Jesus said.
"Write down what I will show you."

And John wrote and WROTE. So we would know what heaven is like.

Heaven!

Where there will be no sin—

No death—

No pain—

And nobody will have to cry any more.

And we will be able to UNDERSTAND ALL THINGS!

But best of all—we will be with JESUS!

IMAGINE!

It's enough to make you dizzy with joy!

And as John thought about the WONDERFUL things Jesus told him about heaven, he must have thought about the last time he had seen Jesus.

John and the other disciples were with Jesus on top of the Mount of Olives when suddenly—Jesus began to rise up in the air before their very eyes—up—up—UP—until a cloud covered him and they couldn't see Him anymore. And while they stood there speechless, two angels appeared and told them that Jesus was coming back some day.

Of course!

John remembered. Jesus had told them before, that He was going to prepare a place for them. In heaven! "I will come back again," Jesus had said. "And until I come, I have a job for you to do. Tell everyone about me. Start where you are and then go out and tell everyone!"

And the disciples did just that. They started in Jerusalem— right where they were. They told people and told them and TOLD them.

"Jesus is alive!"

"He's coming back someday!"

"And someday—SOMEDAY—everyone who trusts Jesus as Saviour will live in heaven WITH Jesus!"

O Joy!

319

Tracy and Mike Talk It Over

Mike: That's so SUPER I can hardly stand it. That's the most super thing I ever heard.

Tracy: I know. My dad says it boggles your mind.

Mike: My dad says it BLOWS your mind.

Tracy: My mom says it takes your breath away.

Mike: I think it all means the same thing. Just think! Someday we're going to be with JESUS!

Tracy: I can hardly wait!

Mike: Jesus doesn't want us to just sit around waiting—He gave us a job to do. We're suppose to tell people about Him.

Tracy: Where could we go to tell all the people?

Mike: We don't have to go anywhere. We can start right here where we are!

Have your puppets take it from here. Suggest ways they can spread the news: start where they are, at home, in school, with their neighbors, etc. And they can help spread the good news all over the world by giving to the work of missionaries, praying for them, etc.

Some Bible Verses to Learn

God . . . loved us and sent his Son. 1 John 4:10
You will be my witnesses. Acts 1:8

Talk to God

Thank God for sending Jesus to be our Saviour. Thank Him for the promise that all who trust Jesus as Saviour will someday live in heaven with Him. Ask God to help you do your part in telling everyone about Jesus.

Can You Find This Story in the Bible?

Find Revelation 1:1-20; Acts 1:8-11; John 14:1-3.

Tracy and Mike
Puppets

1. Cover puppets with clear Contact paper and cut out.

2. Cut slits and fasten as shown. A piece of tape may be added to hold tabs more firmly.

3. Slide puppet over one finger and move to indicate speaking/action. If one child is using both puppets, put a puppet on each hand.

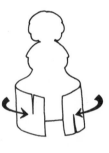